My *Pink* STILETTOS

Presented By

Dr. Larita Rice-Barnes

My Pink Stilettos

Copyright © 2020

Dr. Larita Rice-Barnes

Printed in the United States of America

Library of Congress – Catalogued in Publication Data

ISBN 13-978-1-7359819-0-1

Publication Services

My Pink Stilettos

(A Division of Global Impact Leadership Alliance)
www.resetyourlife2.com

1. Inspirational
2. Women's Issues
3. Depression in the Church

Unless noted, all scriptures are from the
King James Version of the Bible.

Foreword

"My Pink Stilettos," is more than just a title but a much-needed book led by **Dr. Larita Rice-Barnes**. It is also a reminder of women who love the Lord. There are still people in the 21st century trying to make the case that women should never be in leadership worldwide. But there were **22 Fearless Women in the Bible:**

1. **Sarah**

2. **Ruth**, the Moabite

3. **Priscilla** ministered the Gospel together with her husband, Aquila.

4 **Mary Magdalene** was delivered from a life of demonic oppression and experienced the resurrected power of Christ.

5. **Hannah** is one of the most inspiring women in the Bible and also one of the most identifiable women in Scripture for a number of reasons. We recognize her for her sorrow. She wanted a child so badly but was barren. She prayed to God to be granted a son and in return, promised to dedicate his life to the service of God.

6. The **Samaritan Woman**

7. **Mary of Bethany**

8. **Queen Esther** is an inspiring story about a remarkable woman willing to risk her life to save her people.

9. **Jehosheba**, daughter of King Joram, gripped by the power of motherly instinct, fled danger to protect her son from death and helped preserve Israel's future.

10. **Deborah** is known for her wisdom, courage, and compassionate zeal for justice. She was also known as a Prophet and Judge to Israel.

11. Moses' sister **Miriam** displays remarkable intelligence and confidence. She helped to save her brother's life and helped set Israel's deliverance in motion.

12. **Achsah,** in the Bible, is the daughter of Joshua's friend Caleb (Joshua 15:16). Caleb promises his daughter Achsah to whoever takes the town, and Othniel, Kenaz's son, takes on the challenge.

13. **Daughters of Phillip the Evangelist,** these four single young women had the gift of prophecy, and their ministry is mentioned in the Book of Acts. They represent boldness, courage, and a willingness to step out for the Lord, no matter the season of life. They were highly esteemed.

14. **Mary, mother of Jesus, i**s one of the most admired figures in Scripture and considered by many to be the greatest of all Christian saints.

All of these women experienced some fear at some point – it's part of being human. Yet, no matter how overwhelmed that fear may have made them feel, they were able to break through and become change-agents because of it. These fearless women may have lived in completely different societies and times than us, but can surprisingly teach us a great deal from their stories.

I have learned how hard **Dr. Larita Rice-Barnes** works. She is very passionate about her work and very highly organized. Dr. Barnes is a genuine people-person, a true leader. She is one of these women. She knows how to put her work first in all that she does or plans to do to make changes in her community work and her outreach ministry.

Goodwill Ambassador Dr. Lenora Peterson-Maclin

Chief Executive, Global of International Alliance Online School Programs

Ambassador for 44th President Barak Obama

The National Community Services for People of Choice

USA -Chairperson for Ladies Of All Nation Int'l UK

Endorsements

Apostle Larita, thanks for being a Phenomenal Woman --Leading, Guiding, Training, and Creating New Footprints. You are not afraid to step out to change the atmosphere.

-Suzy D. Douglas

There are so many wonderful things I could say about Apostle Larita Barnes, but my favorite thing about her is that her hands are clean, and her heart is pure. She is full of integrity, wisdom, compassion, and love. She's such a special gift to the Body of Christ, and I am honored to have the opportunity to call her my sister!

-Dr. Kia Kia

Dedication

This book is dedicated to all of the women across the globe that have been touched by pain. Pain has no discrimination. In most cases, we absolutely have no control over how it will hit us. Some of you have never experienced being cheated on, physically or sexually abused, kicked to the side, or left for dead. You may have never even experienced any financial struggles. But, we all, at some point in our life, have felt pain. At some point in life, we all have had to face the reality of who we are. We have had to take a deep dive into our souls and examine the dark spots. The places that we have tucked away are so deep. They include places of low self-esteem; And the hidden things that we hide from others, but we know that they exist. We paint our faces with expensive cosmetics. We dress up in our St. John suits and put on our red bottoms. In a lot of cases, we are hiding behind masks. My prayer is that you will continue to dig deep and rise high. Do the inner work that is necessary to become the absolute best version of yourself.

To my sisters that have done the work and seemingly, somehow life has still hit, I'm praying for you. To my sisters who have been touched with a physical ailment, I'm praying for you. To all of my sisters that have felt the knife of a surgeon, you've set in a chemo chair, you've undergone dialysis, the doctor's report still hasn't been favorable, or they haven't told you that you can ring the bell, please know that your

Pink Stilettos Sisters are standing tall with you and praying for you. We are decreeing the power of healing over your life. May your faith be ever increased. May your mind be empowered to envision yourself leaping and running with joy. I want to leave you with this scripture.

Now unto him, that is able to keep you from falling, and to present you faultless before the presence of his glory with exceeding joy, To the only wise God our Saviour, be glory and majesty, dominion and power, both now and ever. Amen. Jude 24-25 (King James Version)

Acknowledgments

God has been good to me. He has been faithful to ME!! He has been ever present with me. If I had ten thousand tongues, I COULD NOT thank him enough!! He has carried me through the storms of life and he has allowed me to live to tell about it.

I am eternally gratefully for every person that have played a part to bring my vision to past. I could NOT have pulled this off without you. Thank you to my sister, Sharmee Pratt. She has been a confidante, prayer partner, friend and a watchman on the wall.

Apostle Barbara McClain stepped right in every time along this journey. You know some of the deepest parts of my trauma that I have encountered and yet you still remain present. I love you! My sister, Dr. Missy you were at the beginning of this project and a part of the conversations to help me release, think, regroup and gather myself for next steps along the way. I'm forever grateful.

I've been blessed to encounter some amazing women who have become my sisters. They entered my life as confirmations of the next place that God was launching me to. Let's first start with Lisa Nicole Cloud. Your invitation to share my story on your stage re-ignited my passion and love to work with women. Your love for your family and your vision to see women win is contagious. I couldn't say thank you enough. Making that drive to Atlanta the first time, was one of the best things that I could have ever done. It afforded me some strong relationships that to this day continue to flourish. I met Ambassador Dr. Lenora Peterson who has claimed me as her own. Dr. Lenora you are simply amazing! One of a kind. You are a complete blessing to the body of Christ and the world. You have paved the way and opened so many doors for many across the globe including me. Thank you for seeing me. Thank you for believing in me and trusting me to walk with you. I am forever grateful.

Dr. Missy Johnson whom I've already mentioned, was at the same event. Next there was De'Iona Monay who is like a daughter/sister. Your skills and drive are amazing. We have traveled across the Trans-Atlantic Ocean together. Thank you for trusting me. Then there was my sister, Lethia Owens. The Audacity of Faith brought us together for a purpose far greater than either one of us can imagine. You were my blessing in disguise. You became one of my main wedding coordinators along with Sharmee and my daughter. You held the key to my hidden treasures that I had prayed for literally. When the time came with no reserve, you unlocked the box. I literally went shopping in your basement for crystal, glass rhinestones, vases, beautiful flowers and more for my wedding. God had you hold on to all of those things and more for at least two years waiting on us to connect. My wedding was absolutely beautiful. So many of you joined forces to make it everything that I had hoped for. And then there's my childhood friend Janice Hundley who I know made her husband get on a plane and fly to be with us. Lol. Thank you for your friendship over the years. We've cried together, laughed together and even wrestled together literally. By the way I'm no longer looking for my eye. Lol. Dr. Keia Simmons you are one amazing young lady. You are my God is dope twin! Yes, he is! He knows how to bring a plan together. He knows when to connect us together. Thank you for always being battle ready! Keep soaring, keep allowing God to separate the wheat from the tare. Divine connections will be your new normal. You have been handpicked and selected by God! Love you sissy!

To my Maid of Honor, Sylvia O'neal. I love you. You prophesied to me about my husband long before he and I had connected to date. When you spoke a word from God, I listened. We have weathered a lot of storms together. You became my first realtor to secure the house that God had for me and through that transaction I gained a sister forever. Thank you for being consistent. Your family is my family.

To my Empowerment of Grace Leadership team and family, I am grateful for your love and support. When God uprooted me from Illinois, EOG core group held it down. The women were forced to a new place of glory. Prophet Suzy Douglas, Amber J. Kenyaetta, Elder Carolyn Rice-Smith, Canesha J, you ladies are true giants in the kingdom of God. You are the most hardest working and dedicated women I've ever had the pleasure of working with in ministry. You are prayer warriors, intercessors, prophetic watchman and gatekeepers. I am what I am ministerially because you were. You allowed me to travel the world to carry out what God called me to do. When things didn't make sense spiritually, you guys still believed in me. When transitions and shifts happened, you still followed me as I followed Christ. Months before the global pandemic of COVID-19 happened, God had already moved us out of the building and into streets. He had us at the forefront. It didn't totally make sense to us then. But, it does now. Thank you for being trailblazers, fire starters and generals in the kingdom of God.

In ministry you need people that you can look to and walk with. As a woman it is good to see another woman that is living out their purpose and calling. Dr. Cynthia Hale, Senior Pastor and Founder of the Ray of Hope Church was just that. I met her several years ago when she was preaching and dancing. I was stunned by her beautiful and her powerful message. She and I later connected. She allowed me into her ELAH program. Your example of being a woman in power and clarity of purpose is beautiful. We can find you on the front lines or speaking or praying at the Democratic Convention. Thank you for setting an example on how one can do justice. When we talk I am enlightened and empowered. You allowed me in your circle and I am grateful.

We need women warrior justice fighters and my sister, Dr. Cassandra Gould, is just that. We became sisters at the right time. What an honor it was to walk the streets with you protesting and rallying for justice. Where I come from, social justice and being a Christian don't mix. I was told that you have to keep them separate. You enforced my beliefs that the two definitely go together. Your strength and courage to fight even when tanks and tear gas was being released gave fuel to those that had become weakened. It was you that made the call to FIA to call for help to come to Ferguson, Mo, after Michael Brown was killed. I love you sis. May everything that belongs to you in this season be released in Jesus name!

To Ciera Bates-Chamberlain, thanks for your friendship and most of all for you seeing my gifts and allowing me to serve. You trusted God and your instincts and hired me on right in the middle of a pandemic. You helped change the trajectory of my financial destiny. I've dreamt for over 20 years about getting paid for what I love to do. I love community and I absolutely love being a voice and presence to those that are marginalized. You entered my life at the right time and I will never forget you. To my Live Free and Faith in Action family you all have welcomed me into the fold with open arms. I'm grateful for every training and every resource that I have been afforded. It is because of you all that the work I had only dreamt of for over 20 years was able to take its greater form. I love you all forever.

Everyone needs a support system. My family has been just that. I wouldn't have made it into this world without my parents. My mother, Carolyn Rice-Smith is actually one of the authors for this project. She is a prayer warrior, prophetic voice, intercessor, gatekeeper and the list goes on. Mom, you have been my strength and my legs. When I couldn't make it to certain assignments you would avail yourself every time. I love you always. To my beautiful daughters, Canesha and Camille, mommy loves you with every fiber of my being. EVERY thing that I do, I have you in mind. I want the legacy that I leave to be rich. I want every day of your lives to be 1 billion times brighter and more powerful than anything I've ever accomplished and anything that the both of you could ever have imagined for yourselves.

To my amazing husband, friend, confidante, lover and side-kick. Mr. Juard M. Barnes, I love you forever. From the moment you entered my life, I knew that there was something about you that would literally sweep me off my feet and it did. Baby, you have been my rock. My shoulder to cry on and ears to listen even when I myself didn't know what I was trying to say. There is no way in the world I would be able to do a pinch of what I do in your absence. It is because of the gift you are in every area, I'm able to be who I am fully and unapologetically. Thank you for our amazing sons and grandchildren that you have given me. They are so talented and so loving. They have welcomed me and the girls in the family with open arms. Juard and Cameron I pray over you often. I give God thanks for your brilliance. I'm front row and center waiting to see what the next multimillion dollar idea will be. I can't wait to spend more time with the both of you.

To every prayer warrior, intercessor, prophetic watchman on the wall that has stood with me and for me on my journey, you know who you are and I am forever grateful. Now to the woman who helped me and my mom to become the women we are today. My Gramma. My personal superstar and our champion. It was your deep love for your family that has been instilled in me to this day. Your compassion, your wittiness, your brilliance and talent has been hidden in my heart. You possessed strength and poise like no other. Always praying and being present for others. Only if you were here today to witness the deliverance and breakthrough that has happened in our immediate family. It was you that encouraged me through your style to come out of my long sleeves and skirts. You allowed me to grab pieces from your closet even though they were too big. You even let me walk around in some of your heels at times flopping off of my feet. Today I send this message to you in heaven that I didn't die in the bondage. The grave clothes have been removed. I've changed my circle of friends. I have a new tribe now Gramma.

To every woman that has ever been in any type of bondage, felt any type of pain, been ostracized or criticized, or received a negative doctor's report, I'm praying for you. I believe in you. I want you to know that no matter how much you have lost, or how deep you have fallen, you too can rise again. It's time to live again, shine again, do it again. Revisit the vision again. I love you with all of my heart.
-Your Pink Stiletto Sister

Table of Contents

CHAPTER 1

WAIT FOR IT

BY DR. LARITA RICE-BARNES

Your Purpose Is Far Greater Than What You Can See Right Now

It has been quite some time since I wrote to you; almost 10 years to be exact. I didn't realize it had been so long until I recently contacted my first publisher to receive copies of my paperwork. I must admit, it was never my intent to take this long to publish another book. I must also report to you that so much has changed. My first published book, "Trapped in the System" was just an introduction to some snippets of my life. I was in my metamorphosis stage just like the caterpillar nearing the end of one life cycle, preparing to enter another one. The manuscript provided a distinct intersectionality of the many detours and roadways that I had to travel. I like to refer to it with a message that I preached several years ago entitled, "I had to Go That Way!" Let's be clear, one of the major things I have learned in life is that NOTHNG just happens. As crazy as that may sound, everything, abso-lutely everything is used for the glory of the Most High. Every intricate part of your story becomes life's classroom in your present and a launching pad for greatness into your future. Every inch of your pain is somehow earmarked and reward-ed. It is true that in our humanness there is only so much we can handle. But through the divine power of our Maker and Creator, there is nothing we cannot overcome.

When I first set out to do, "My Pink Stilettos" co-authoring project, it was 2017. At that time, I talked to one of my friend girls, Dr. Missy Johnson of Fearless Women Rock and told her my thoughts about the book, along with what I was looking to accomplish. She referred me to a publisher that she had previously connected with. In June 2017, I began convers-ing with the publisher and the process began. We started planning how I wanted the book cover to look while discuss-ing the best options for publication. It definitely had to be a quick turnaround. After all, I wanted the book to be released in October 2017 in commemoration of Breast Cancer Aware-ness month. So, I immediately started marketing the project. I got a lot of buzz from individuals that showed interest. I began having conversations and planning for the book re-lease which was just over 90 days away. As soon as it felt like we were getting a good rhythm with people making verbal commitments the unfathomable happened. On August 11, 2017, I was on my way to a women's conference in Detroit, Michigan. I received a call from a young girl screaming my name, "Ms. Larita, Ms. Larita, they're taking Camille to jail." My heart felt like it had dropped to the ground and was im-mediately buried. My mind had to be flying or swimming or sinking one million miles per second. I know that may seem a little weird by description. However, the point is this, all in one split second everything that I had ever known seemingly went blank.

One half of me began to ask, where was she located during the time of the call. The other half of me immediately began to head to the police station to be present and available for my then 13-year-old daughter. I was COMPLETELY speechless and in shock. Numbness had to have set in my whole body. My daughter was an honor roll student, never had been in a fight and was a super respectful and respected young lady. When my oldest daughter and I got to the police station we were greeted with pure rudeness. Couldn't readily get any answers to why she had even been taken into custody. Secondly, she was a minor, why would she even be taken to an adult jail, and thirdly, before they even left the scene of a public park why did they not call me? They arrested her while also leaving my 7 year old niece behind that had been under her care. The officers NEVER called me to say anything. About one week and a half later, I was sexually groped by one of the officers and my oldest daughter, and one of her friends were being pulled over seemingly every week or so by the same police department. It did not stop there. We were harassed too. They would constantly ride by our house slowly and park behind our house on the street behind us. They even showed up at our house a few times in the wee hours of the morning banging on our door for no reason. I remember thinking, if they are going to kill me or harm me, they would have to come in this house and get me. I AM NOT OPENING THE DOOR! Oh, I didn't mention, one day, my daughter and I were parked in our driveway and one of the officers pulled up behind us. He wanted nothing except to intimidate us and utilize gas lighting efforts to wear us down. We were forced to move. I had to withdraw my daughter out of school and began homeschooling. One of the officers that was present at the park while the arrest was happening was an officer at her school.

I was even forced to walk away from one of my cleaning contracts. The police would sit across the lot from the building to just harass us constantly. I ultimately had to walk away from my business of 17 years for more reasons than one. Some days the load just felt too heavy to bear. I remember crying and wondering, "Why, Lord? Why is this happening?" It seemed as though we were doing all the right things to be the model citizen and upright Christian, but yet, this trial had seemingly come to WIPE US OUT! One day distinctly, I decided I couldn't take it anymore. I was balled up on the floor rocking and screaming to the top of my lungs. "I CAN'T take this anymore." It felt like I was dying a slow death all while feeling like my mind was literally being ripped apart. I can vividly remember my oldest daughter somehow ended up at the apartment. She got down on the floor and began to pray and decree life, peace and strength over me. I'm almost sure that she was praying and travailing to the top of her lungs.

However, the words sounded so faint. I could tell that she had made a phone call and was talking to someone about me and the warfare that I was experiencing on the floor. The prayers and fervor increased, and then there was another voice ringing in the air. It was that of Apostle Barbara Mc-Clain. To some, she's Apostle Mama and to me, she's Mama B. Now understand, I have had issues with locking into this whole spiritual mother, spiritual father thing because I was a victim of spiritual rape. But listen, EVERYBODY needs a midwife, an intercessor, a prophetic watchman on the wall to help guard and cover their soul. She has been just that. A confidante, sister-friend, road dog, and just plain genuine and loving, the whole while that I have known her. My daughter obviously knew that she could trust the God in her to help usher in my breakthrough. Mama B's voice began to speak through the phone. The words were piercing. If memory serves me right, she was saying things like daughter, GET UP, You shall not die but live, I cover your mind, I cover your body, and the rest is just too vague.

My daughter knew that I was in a war for my life and my mind. She called for back-up. You see in life we must know when to call for back up. There are some things that we must do alone with God and then there are other things that require us to have some back-up. Just like this book project, *My Pink Stilettos*. I knew that I was not supposed to author this book alone. I knew that there were other women that were called to share this platform with me. You see, in 2017, up until now, so much has been revealed to me. I learned who was real and who was fake. I learned a deeper meaning of what justice, righteousness and equality is. My life seemingly took a turn. I had just reunited with my now husband. He and I at the time of these occurrences had been conversing for almost a year. We had not seen each other prior or communicated in about three years. Then one day, he wrote me and said that he was in town at a COGIC Convention and that he had some people that he wanted me to meet. The convenience of this is that a contract that I had just picked up was actually up the street from the location of where he was. The other thing that was intriguing is that our church had literally been fasting and praying everyday straight 2-3 times per day for about 120 days. God had told us that he was putting our names in the mouths of those that have influence. He was dropping us in new circles, and that He was creating stages and platforms so that we could share our stories. It literally happened almost instantly. I received an email from one of my now sisters, Lisa Nicole Cloud. It went something like this, "Lisa is inviting you to share your story on her stage." Keep in mind, the words that God had spoken to us during our prayer and fasting time. I was floored. Wait. What? I hadn't gotten an email from Lisa in years, and the way that I was introduced to her initially was through another lady that was a part of a multi-level marketing company. It had nothing to do with sharing a stage and was all by a conference line. But, however, or whatever, God's word was being manifested. Just like when God spoke to me during this time and told me to let my guards down to let in male energy to prepare myself for my husband. And I did, then Juard

M. Barnes appeared. The conversations kept going, our love kept growing, and then we became two "barn" into one. Two "barn" into one was one of our wedding tags that we used.

Everything happens in the fullness of time. Although he and I met three years prior, and we had a few conversations at the farm where we met, when he showed up again, it was the right time. My heart was open and my mind was prepared to receive him. He entered my life in what had become a critical time. He is what you would call a gladiator. He loves hard, stands for justice and equality for the most vulnerable and he constantly is at the frontline of things that matter most to changing the world, while shaping this idea of a Global Culture of Health. He is by far the most formidable man that I have ever encountered in my entire life. His strength, his wisdom and guidance have been absolutely everything any woman that is going through some trials could ever hope for. His presence is undeniable and has definitely served as a scaffolding and a solid foundation all in one for me.

This is what I want to talk about next. The importance of a solid foundation. Throughout my life, at the most unpredictable times, God has always somehow allowed me to be thrust onto a solid foundation. One that has kept me from sinking and slipping when the storms of life came beating upon me like a mighty rushing wind. Whenever you begin to research what a foundation is, you will find consistent definitions everywhere. You will discover that a good foundation is crucial to the stability of any structure. In the midst of writing this, I stumbled across a website called SA Homes. I have cited the website for reference. Here is what they had to say about foundations. *"According to the construction experts and engineers, the foundation must be able to withstand the "dead" load and "live" loads. The dead load is the weight or the load of the basic structure itself. This is called dead load as it remains constant. On the other hand, the live load is the weight of the people and other objects that they bring with them. The foun-*

dation must be firm and must be able to channel the weight of the entire building to the ground. If the building is being constructed on sloping regions or moist ground, the foundation has to be customized and durable." https://sahomes.in/blog/the-importance-of-strong-foundations-for-buildings/

When I read this, I could do nothing but laugh. I thought about the fact that I was currently inside of my home in one of the rooms that I frequent most. I then realized that there were walls surrounding me and at least two stories of ceilings over my head. My mind instantly shifted to the fact that myself and others were currently in the house and had been walking around all day. Not once did the house shift or shake. As I'm sitting here typing these words, I'm sitting in a high chair and the floor is not sinking. Foundation is everything. That is the reason I believe God wanted this particular book to be a co-authoring project. He knew that many hands lighten the load, but also that the foundation of this project needed to be wide, deep and sure. There are a couple of scriptures that come to mind. For the context of this writing, I will reference the King James Version (KJV). The first one is found in St. Luke 6:48. It says, *"He is like a man which built an house, and digged deep, and laid the foundation on a rock: and when the flood arose, the stream beat vehemently upon that house, and could not shake it: for it was founded upon a rock." Christ is that solid foundation.* According to my beliefs, everything that we need is found in Him. Each one of the women that is a part of this project was handpicked. Yes, I had a conversation with the Heavenly Father. This project wasn't to be just transactional, but relational. A tribe of women who were committed to building sisterhood and changing the world. See everyone needs somebody. Having someone that is like-minded is priceless. Each and every one of these women have powerful stories of thriving, surviving, overcoming and conquering.

The next scripture that I would like to reference is found in 1 Corinthians 3:13-14. *"Every man's work shall be made manifest: for the day shall declare it, because it shall be revealed by fire; and the fire shall try every man's work of what sort it is. If any man's work abide which he hath built thereupon, he shall receive a reward."* In my opinion this project has been through the fire. The year 2017 was the seed planting year for it. The seed has been germinating ever since, and in 2020, we entered into the fullness of time. We are literally in the midst of a declared global pandemic. Many lives have been affected. On March 11, 2020, the World Health Organization declared the Novel Coronavirus Disease, namely COVID-19 a pandemic. This phenomenon will definitely be written about in some type of history book. What also will be written about is how the amazing co-authors of My Pink Stilettos came together from across the world to pen this masterpiece. They are from everywhere. Africa, Asia, Europe, South America and North America and many cities, states and countries in between.

We are also currently in the midst of one of the most critical elections of my lifetime. The racial tension is high. Black bodies are still being lynched; and Brown bodies, like blacks are still underserved. This book is a prophetic piece speaking to the power of a woman. The power of sisterhood and the power of collaboration. Right now, in the USA, we have just received the first nomination and acceptance from a Woman of Color (WOC) for Vice President of the USA. This is an absolute amazing time to be a woman. To all of my beautiful sisters from all over the globe that will read these pages, let me restate that. As you are walking through these pages, imagine yourself in the best pair of Pink Stilettos that you can think of. Imagine yourself holding hands with every woman that is a part of this book. I want you to know that you have found your tribe. Your tribe knows your vibe and your vibe attracts your tribe. You, my beloved, have been simply set up for greatness. Some of you have incurred scars...even literal physical scars. Maybe it was because of the knife of the doctor that pierced your skin. Maybe it was from an emotional, physical, financial or relational scar that seemingly won't go away. I want to leave you with this quote that Holy Spirit gave me while I was preaching a message several years ago. "Scars are an indication of where you come from, not a limitation to where you are going." In commemoration of all of the powerful women that have felt the sting of breast cancer, your tribe is here. We stand with your family and friends. We are committed to sisterhood. The foundation has been built to weather the storm.

I am Mrs. Barnes

#IWokeUpToPurpose

CHAPTER 2

THE EVERLASTING AFTERSHOCKS OF AN EARTHQUAKE:
MY TESTIMONY TO THE EXTRAORDINARY POWER OF LOVE AND KINDNESS

BY DAWN AIRHART-WITTE

"Remember there's no such thing as a small act of kindness. Every act creates a ripple with no logical end." - Scott Adams

believe we meet everyone for a reason. Sometimes it is just to touch our lives for a moment and other times it is for the greatest of life lessons. I am grateful for the opportunity to be included in this book with these truly inspirational women. Larita Rice Barnes is one of my personal heroes and a soul sister in the truest sense of the word. When she asked me to be a part of this project, I immediately said yes, not knowing any of the details. I will follow her anywhere and my answer to her will always be yes.

The day before our submission deadline for this book, I received a reminder that the first draft of my chapter was due in a little over twenty-four hours. My first thought was, "Uh oh, I don't even know what I am going to write about. I thought I had another two weeks. Yikes." I had visitors from out of town, many deadlines I was working to meet, and a relatively full schedule for the next few days. After a brief moment of panic, I reminded myself that panicking and worrying will not get my chapter written, so I asked God, my Angels, and the Universe to guide me to write something which would touch as many hearts as possible. No more than a few minutes passed, and the answer came to me. This story has been in my heart and soul for over twenty-six years. I share it with you now because it was during this very magical week that I learned a powerful lesson that I felt deep within my soul. It confirmed all I believe in the extraordinary power of LOVE.

I want to share one of my most beautiful experiences of unconditional love, kindness, inspiration, and continued blessings that was born out of tragedy. On January 17, 1994, Los Angeles was jolted awake by a 6.7 magnitude earthquake at 4:30 in the morning. I had been through several milder earthquakes while living in Southern California, but the Northridge earthquake was by far the biggest. Earthquakes quite literally shake our very foundations. They are unlike storms that we can see approaching. There is little we can do to prepare for their shock. If you experienced this earth-quake, then I am sure you will remember it as if it just hap-pened. As I usually did after an earthquake, I immediately turned on the television to hear the reports of the magnitude and impact. I could not believe the devastation I was seeing once the reporters were on the scene. A portion of the 10 Freeway, one of the busiest and largest freeways in the coun-try, had collapsed. A parking garage in a shopping mall had trapped a security officer underground. Thousands of apart-ments, condos and houses were destroyed or left uninhabit-able, leaving thousands of people homeless. My heart broke seeing the tremendous devastation. Knowing that so many people's lives were affected, while my family and I were safe and secure, made me want to do something to help but I didn't know what.

For days, the news continued to show the devastation all around us. My fear of earthquakes grew because I had two young daughters, dogs, and cats I needed to protect. Earth-quakes will surely happen again and what if we were in a store or on the freeway or.... the list went on and on in my mind, but thankfully, greater than my fear was my empathy. I felt so deeply for those who were suffering. I did not real-ize it at the time, but instead of focusing on my fears, I shift-ed my focus on how I could be of service to help someone else in their time of need. After all, that could have been me and my family left without a home. What would I have done? Where would my family have gone? I needed to help another mother who had suffered the loss I was grateful to have been spared. I always remember one of my favorite quotes from Princess Diana, "Carry out a random act of kindness, with no expectation of reward, safe in the knowledge that one day someone might do the same for you." The devastation left by the earthquake was definitely a time that I felt called to kindness.

My house is comfortable, but not terribly large. Because my daughters were very young, we only used a few rooms because we were always in close proximity. We had two bedrooms and a bathroom that we did not use much, so I thought I could offer those rooms to a family who needed them. This was well before the Internet, so I could not just google a number to find a place to offer my home. I am not even sure what I would have googled if it had existed. One day I saw an 800 FEMA number on the news, and unbeknownst to my former husband, I called and offered our two bedrooms to provide safe harbor for a family who lost their home in the earthquake until they got back on their feet. They added my name to a list and thanked me for my call. I had no idea anything was going to come of it until I received a call about a week later. The lovely woman on the phone told me she and her husband had two sons, ages six and nine. They had lost their apartment and nearly all of their belongings in the earthquake. We had a brief conversation and after explaining that I lived with a few dogs and more cats than I care to admit, we arranged for her and her husband to come over and meet us. Before we ended that call, I remember her asking me if I was a Christian. I told her that I embrace all faiths because love and kindness have always been my highest calling. No matter what our religion, God always knows our hearts. I was excited that I was going to be able to help someone who needed it but now I had to tell my then husband. To my amazement, he was not all that surprised that I would do such a thing and was open to the idea. I told my mom and my mother-in-law; they both thought I was a crazy.

Sharing your home with a friend in need is one thing but a family of complete strangers may have seemed "crazy" to some. To me, it was the most natural thing in the world to do. Mister Rogers reminded us to "look for the helpers," and I have always wanted to be one of the helpers. I certainly could not control the earthquake, but I surely could help people whose lives were impacted by it.

John and Merrilyn moved into our home with their two precious boys at the beginning of February 1994. They had lost most of their belongings in the earthquake and had very little to actually move. But they had each other, they had their faith, and now they had us. Having four adults, four children, four dogs, and at least eight cats in one house was quite an adventure for all of us. Merrilyn and I got to know one another, and I adored having them all here. We cooked dinners together. We shared recipes and family stories. About a month after they arrived, one of the boys came down with the chicken pox, followed a few days later by his brother and then my two daughters. Four children with chicken pox in one home was quite the experience. It was an extraordinary few months, to say the least. Although it came with some challenges, we survived and came out better for the experience.

Our new family members found a house to rent and were able to furnish it modestly and start rebuilding their life in early April. I was so happy that things were better for them and I was sad to see them go, but I knew we had made friends for life. Friends who were family. We were invited to a house-warming party shortly after they were settled into their new home and I got to meet the extended family. We felt welcomed and tremendously loved. I could feel the sincere gratitude from the entire family for the kindness and love we had extended. Any small challenge we had encountered was insignificant compared to how it felt knowing that I had made a real difference in the lives of others. One of my very favorite quotes is by Ralph Waldo Emerson and he says, "To laugh often and much; To win the respect of intelligent people and the affection of children; To earn the appreciation of honest critics and endure the betrayal of false friends; To appreciate beauty, to find the best in others; To leave the world a bit better, whether by a healthy child, a garden patch, or a redeemed social condition; To know even one life has breathed easier because you have lived. This is to have succeeded." This is my definition of success. This experience confirmed that to me.

Had this story ended there, it would have been worthy of sharing. The satisfaction I received knowing that another had breathed easier because I existed, and the new friendships I had made, were the greatest rewards I could have received. But what happened twenty-six years later is another reason why I have absolute faith that divine magic exists and that love and kindness are absolutely why we are here.

Shortly after I was asked to be a part of this amazing project, I received a text from the adorable six-year-old that lived in my house for a few months after the earthquake. I had not heard from Garrison for over twenty-five years and I had only kept in touch with his mom a few times since they had moved across the country and our lives got busy. Fortunately, social media had kept us up to date with big milestones in each other's lives and I was so happy to still have that connection. Garrison was no longer six but rather a grown adult of thirty-one. He was in Los Angeles and wanted to see if he could stop by for a visit. My answer was an absolute YES! I was so excited to see him, but I had no idea what to expect. The moment he walked in the door it was if no time had passed. He was no longer an adorable six-year-old boy, but he was now a handsome thirty-one-year-old man. Garrison had his beautiful girlfriend, now my newest soul friend, Kylie, with him. It felt like we had always been connected and that no time had passed. Although now he was a grown man who towered over me, I still saw the precious little boy I knew so long ago.

The first day they arrived, we talked well into the night. Garrison told me how that time felt to him as a six-year-old child. He explained to me that the kindness I extended to him and his family had made the most profound impact on him and his entire family. Kylie told me that she knew about me because of how often Garrison would talk about me. I sat in disbelief because, although I knew I had extended a kindness, I had no idea how deeply I had impacted their lives and touched their souls. The following is from Garrison:

"No words are sufficient enough to emphasize the change in my family's life from one seemingly small act of kindness. We are forever in debt to what we know as the kindest family on earth. That kindness has forever been a seed planted in my heart that has manifested itself throughout the years to every single person that I have come into contact with. At the tender age of six, the kindness of one special and beautiful family, the phone call of one lovely, caring mother, left such an impression on my little heart, that nothing in this dark cruel world could take away. At the age of thirty-one, I still remember what was done for me and how it shaped me into the man that I am today. There is something to be said about genuine, deep, unconditional love and kindness... their abiding and constant results are inestimable and grand!" ~ Garrison Haywood

The gift I received from Garrison not only filled my soul with such unconditional love, it was yet another confirmation in my life that love, and kindness are exactly why we are here. It also reaffirmed my belief that each act of love we extend to another living soul is magnified and amplified out into the universe so far-reaching and vast that we may never know the true impact our love can have. To know that by my example another soul understands the profound impact we can have on another is why I am here and why I do all that I do.

I am so proud of the young man that Garrison has grown up to be. He is a tremendous father who loves his beautiful daughter, Abigail. He is thoughtful, kind, considerate, insightful, intelligent and much more. To know that I had even a tiny role in shaping how this amazing man sees the world...that is a gift greater than any treasure.

The divine timing of this project with Garrison and Kylie's visit was in no way a coincidence. I do not believe in coincidences, but rather synchronicities. Many people will come into our lives throughout our lifetime. There are lessons to be learned in every interaction and experience we have. When we look for the purpose in all, we will find it. Strangers are only strangers until we say hello. When we live our lives full of love and kindness that is exactly what we will receive in return.

CHAPTER 3

DEPRESSION IN THE CHURCH

BY YOLONDA GAYDEN

Depression is defined as a mood disorder that causes a persistent feeling of sadness and a loss of interest which affects how you feel, think, and behave and can lead to a variety of emotional and physical problems. Depression is a disorder that must be diagnosed by a medical professional and it can affect the strongest of individuals. This is an account of my own personal struggle with depression as I learned a lot about myself and people close to my heart. It will recount how I battled with what is commonly known as a sickness. No two encounters may be the same and anyone that believes that they are experiencing depression should seek help from a medical professional as well as stay diligent in prayer.

Being a faithful member in the church, as well as a studious Sunday school student and midweek service attendee, I was always thrilled to be at church. I was adamant about worship and being in right relationship with God. My story may be different from most in that during this time I had no events going on in my life that could be considered stressful or negative. For the most part, life was good, and it seemed as if God was answering my prayers. I was at peace and content with my present situation. There was nothing going on that would cause a downward slide into depression. Aside from this, depression was an issue that was rarely discussed in the church and was for, the most part, a taboo subject among Christians. The common perception was that there must be something wrong in your walk with Christ if God was allowing the enemy to attack you in this way.

The reality is that church folk are not exempt from the attack of depression. My pastor at the time was of the school of thought that, "Saints don't get depressed." Although I harbor no ill will against him for this line of thinking and have the utmost respect for his leadership capabilities, I now know that he lacked adequate information to be more effective in speaking about the matter. The idea that something is lacking in your Christian walk is still a commonly held belief.

Before I realized what was going on, I started forgetting things -- a lot of things. This symptom was not likely age-related because I was only 24-years old at the time. I started feeling pressure in my head that was relentless. I began having mood swings that were uncontrollable and frequent. Since everyone experiences depression in different ways, there is no single remedy for the sickness. Thus, it is advisable that we remain sensitive and nonjudgmental of our fellow believers.

Identifying Signs of Depression

I can recall one day in particular, while running errands, feeling that my brain was in a fog. As I entered the large retail store, I hadn't the slightest idea why I had come there. To no avail, I struggled to remember. I was also going through periods of not sleeping well. I was often sad and unable to focus clearly and complete routine tasks. I had little interest in socializing. My appetite was poor, and I began to gain weight. The feeling of hopelessness and despair seemed constant. I had trouble falling asleep. When I did, I slept too much. I felt as though I were a failure in life and experienced overwhelming feelings of guilt.

I decided to talk to my doctor. I explained to him everything that was going on and he told me that I was experiencing depression. My immediate reply was, "The devil is a liar!" Not me, a saved, chosen, and faithful servant of the Lord. "God's people don't get depressed," or so I thought. His response to me was, "Okay, the devil is a liar in a lot of things, but you are dealing with depression." Although I heard the words of the doctor, I remained in disbelief as he suggested medication, and I refused. I could not bring myself to believe I was suffering from depression. It is not uncommon for those suffering to be in denial about their condition. I refused to acknowledge that God would allow this to happen to His servant. Sometimes I think we often forget that "Saints" are not exempt from going through trials and tribulations. After a short time, my condition did not seem to be getting better. I decided to talk about it to others. I first mentioned it to my husband who indicated to me that I needed to intensify my prayer life. After this, I actually felt more sadness. I felt as if I were contributing to my own problem. I started to feel as if I were inadequate in my walk and my faith in Christ. I continued to pray and seek God for guidance, even though I felt God was not answering my prayers concerning this fight with depression. I was in a serious battle for my mental health.

All of the symptoms started to intensify in depth and severity. The anxiety, memory loss, lack of focus, poor appetite, and pains in my head and chest continued to grow worse. I continued to feel hopeless and sleep eluded me. I decided to reach out again to a friend that referred me to a seasoned mother in the church that prayed for me. My situation still grew worse. I felt as if I were going to lose my mind. I could not understand how this was happening. I was dumbfounded as to why I was suffering in this way. I continued to pray that God would heal me, even though things seemed to be unbearable.

During this time, I was a stay-at-home mom with two small children. Taking care of a home, children, and a husband became a daunting responsibility. I felt as though I was at my lowest point. I went back to prayer and asked God for direction. I heard the voice of God speaking to me and assuring me that He was still a healer and a deliverer even if I were taking medication. I went back to the doctor and received the medication and started taking it immediately. The medication helped to some degree in staying focused, although the battle was still ongoing.

The pain was there every day. I spent a lot of time crying and trying to understand why I was going through this situation. Every morning after taking my children to school, I would get home and pass out and sleep for hours and later fight to do daily activities at home. I remember my husband and I shared a car and before picking up the children from school, I would pick him up at work to run errands and would sleep while he drove due to the effects of the medication. When his errands were finished, I would sleep in the car at his job until it was time to pick the children up from school. I would pick them up and get home and help with homework and once again, I would fall asleep.

This is not the life I wanted to live. I could not go anywhere or do anything. For seven months, I went through the worse days of my life. I needed the pain and the hurt to stop. I felt like I was not living at all. I felt dead. My life was upside down. This was not the life God had for me. One of the side effects of the medicine was suicidal tendencies. One night I began having suicidal thoughts. A few days later, I went back to the doctor. I was tired and angry. He advised me to stay on the medication.

Lessons learned from Depression

There are many lessons that I learned during my battle with depression. First, I learned that depression is nothing to be ashamed of. This condition found me at a time when things were going smoothly for me and seemingly could not be contributed to any action of mine. Godly people will suffer trials and tribulations also. There was nothing that I did or did not do to cause me to go through depression. I know that God rains on the just as well as the unjust means that good people can have bad things happen to them. During this time, I realized that it was not a good idea to allow myself to be involved with things that could cause sadness, such as sad songs, movies, or depressing television shows. I also found that exercise and physical activity were good to uplift my low spirit. Increasing my self-care with long, hot soaking baths surrounded by candlelight, coupled with meditation, and reading helped to relieve stressful situations. Being a believer brings with it things we will inevitably have to face and deal with on many different levels. Godly people lose their jobs, their wealth, health, and loved ones in tragedies just as unbelievers do.

It was, for me, important to remain faithful to God in one of my deepest trials. I had to learn to have patience and wait on God. I had to endure pain, suffering, persecution, self-infliction, pity, and loneliness. I had to not only pray, but to pray fervently and earnestly and be intentional about having deep, intimate conversations with God. I asked God for what

I needed, and I received in my heart, spirit, and mind, that it was already done. I would then give Him praise and thank Him for bringing it to pass, even when I saw no evidence that my prayers were being answered. I had to trust God in the process. Many times, we say with our mouths that we don't mind waiting but waiting can be as painful as it is long. This trial taught me to hold on to my faith through hurt and hardship. All the things I learned have made me the fighter that I am today. Overall, it helped to increase my faith and allow me to trust God in difficult situations.

Healing and Deliverance

I made a habit of praying daily and nightly. One Sunday, I went to church and while the choir was singing, I heard God say, "Today is your day." I knew God was saying that my healing and deliverance were here. I received the word in my spirit and started crying. The pastor preached, and as soon as the altar call was made, I quickly made my way to the altar and I felt the power of God touch me all over my body. As I closed my eyes, I began thanking God for His power and anointing. I felt the pressure in my head leave and I began to cry even more. I danced and shouted as I continued to allow God to work a miracle in me. I knew that I was healed. I felt a joy that I had never felt before. This was a divine intervention by God and a testament of His power and faithfulness.

Although I would never recommend this to anyone suffering from depression, I stopped taking the medication my doctor had prescribed. He had mentioned on previous occasions that the medicine must be gradually reduced in order for me to get off of it. The rest is history. God did it for me and I was most assuredly healed, and I walk in that healing from God. Twenty-two years have passed, and I have been blessed to be a Lead Teacher at a local university, a motivational speaker, a Certified Life Coach, and a Licensed Evangelist. I am also a co-author of three books. I have participated in discussion panels, women's conferences, and revivals. I am also the founder and CEO of YCG Ministries, a women's ministry empowering women to reach their destiny and full potential in God.

My Battle with Depression Becomes a Promotion

Looking back, I now marvel at how God takes the thing that comes to destroy us and turns it into an antidote to make us stronger and wiser. My fight with depression made me feel overwhelmed and lost. Of all the trials I have encountered in my Christian journey, depression was by far the greatest threat to my physical and spiritual well-being. My prayer life was elevated to a new level in God. My faith was elevated. I believed that there was nothing God could not do! I fasted and prayed to God many times, but on one particular occasion, I fasted three straight days and afterwards felt the presence of God and His power working on my behalf. I was a student of God's Word and knew that when presented with any trial, to use the Word as my weapon. I would read it over and over to allow it to saturate my mind and spirit. I emerged stronger in my walk with God. I had a peace that I did not have before the months of torment.

Depression is a serious condition and should be treated under the guidance of a doctor; however, remaining steadfast in your faith is necessary for believers as well. You can still seek medical attention while waiting on God to heal you. As a believer, keep in mind that deliverance comes in many different ways. For some, deliverance may consist of finding a medication that works well. For some, surgery may be their answer for deliverance. In some of my other battles, deliverance was from taking oral medications and surgery. I am still a firm believer that God heals supernaturally, as He has done for me, from depression as well as other illnesses.

This Means War

Depression is something that comes and turns your world upside down. It is important to make the Word an important factor in your fight with depression. There are biblical principles to help you fight. For strength: Ephesians 6:10, "Finally, my brethren, be strong in the Lord and in the power of His might." II Samuels 22:2-3, "And he said, The Lord is my rock, and my fortress, and my deliverer. The God of my rock; in Him will I trust: He is my shield and the horn of my salvation, my high tower, and my refuge, my savior, thou savest me from violence." Jeremiah 29:11, "For I know the thoughts that I think toward you, saith the Lord, thoughts of peace, and not of evil, to give you an expected end."

My Pink Stilettos
There is Victory after Depression

I am blessed to say, that I fought and won and God caused me to overcome depression. I was able to graduate from Bible College and receive many certifications in the field of Early Childhood. I have participated in stage play productions and I have been featured in an international magazine featuring women in business and in the ministry. There is hope and victory for believers who suffer from depression. There is life after depression. I walk strongly, boldly, and confidently in my purpose and calling while wearing **My Pink Stilettos.**

CHAPTER 4

THE MAKING
OF A WARRIOR:
A PUBLIC PROCESS FOR A
PUBLIC REDEMPTION

BY BRANDI ROJAS

*"Victorious Warriors win first and then go
to war, while defeated warriors go to war
first and then seek to win."*
-Sun Tzu

But when Paul had gathered a bundle of sticks and laid them on the fire, a [viper crawled out because of the heat and fastened itself on his hand. When the natives saw the creature hanging from his hand, they began saying to one another, "Undoubtedly this man is a murderer, and though he has been saved from the sea, Justice [the avenging goddess] has not permitted him to live." Then Paul [simply] shook the creature off into the fire and suffered no ill effects. But they stood watching and expecting him to swell up or suddenly drop dead. But after they had waited a long time and had seen nothing unusual happen to him, they changed their minds and began saying that he was a god."
Acts 28:3-6

There is nothing like being on the other side of your process. Filled with turns and flips, it leads one to ask, "What in the world is going on? What did I do to deserve this?" This question echoed in my mind as I endured the public process of losing what seemed irreplaceable; only for God to redeem it all and more. Everything seemed perfect – the house had just been built and the opportunity arose for me to attend school full time to pursue my dream, and an even bigger opportunity of opening my own studio had finally come true.

In October 2008, I signed the lease expecting the best and disregarding the worst. Dreams overtook silent signs and the smoke of arising warfare. For days and even weeks before my lease signing, I went to the space every day, parked in the back and worshipped God for the favor and breakthrough that He would activate in that place. Many days, I started in my car, but later found myself outside the car with the door open and laying prostrate on the ground. As I prepared for the signing of what seemed to be the dream of my life, all I could remember was what that place represented. You see, many years before, it served as the mall on "our" side of town.

I spent many days as a young girl going to Montgomery Ward and Dillard's with my mother. As she would purchase items and head to the check out, we would be greeted by a cashier whom I always admired. My admiration went beyond the person to what they were operating, a cash register! To me it seemed magical as they pushed buttons and scanned items. My favorite part was watching it open at the end of the transaction and seeing the receipt paper shoot out. This love led me to ask my daddy for a cash register. His response was not to buy me a "play register," but instead to buy the best one he could find. Yes, a real one! As I signed my name on the dotted line, tears streamed down my face at the thought of how God would bring me full circle, from the fascination of the mall to now launching my dream on the same grounds.

At that time, I was not well-versed on spiritual warfare. In fact, I knew nothing about it really. My expectation was that I and we, as this was during the time of my former marriage, would just be free to live our perfect lives without interruption. I remember one day after the opening; someone I had known since a little girl came to visit me. She had a space nearby and came over for a quick visit. As she entered, I ran up to greet her. With a big smile full of optimism, her response remained that of a smirk as she entered the door. As I greeted her, she apologized for missing the grand opening and dedication. She came in, eyes wide open, complimenting me on the space. She walked in slowly and shifted to the far-right wall. As she walked, she kept saying, "Hmmm" and "Oh wow!" She walked around the entire room, running her hands down every wall until it led her back to the door. She looked at me and said, "This is really nice. Good luck," and quickly exited. Full of excitement, I replied, "It means the world to me that you came; you have no idea how much!" She looked back, smirked again, and went back down the walkway. I had no idea then, but years later found out, that she had been hosting meetings about me with others who knew me and had begun placing bets on how long it would be before I lost the space. For weeks, I worked along with one other instructor who taught a group of beautiful children, some of which had been dancing with me for years and others who came in due to the opening of the studio. There were days that we practiced only to end up laying out in the presence of God, unable to move another step because of the weight of His anointing and touch. In these precious moments, God touched babies who never knew Him in that capacity and left them desiring more. Most of them did not know that dance even had the capacity to cause God's attention to be turned to them in that way, but it happened day after day and rehearsal after rehearsal.

While all of this was going on, there was something looming in the background. I could feel it but could not name it. I began to fill the unsettling. The best word I can use is that it felt like the beginning of an earthquake. Many days, depression would just show up and almost swallow me whole. It was on these days especially that I had to lean into the anointing of dance to bring me through. Life all around seemed so rocky, as my sophomore year in college was coming to a close in December 2008. Everything around me began to shake my focus, especially in school and despite my best efforts it was often clouded by the tears of words unspoken and thoughts unable to be conveyed. God had begun to sharpen me in my dance classes for that semester, however, the other classes left me stumped as I fought to keep my studio and my house at peace. As the semester came to a close, I released a deep sigh, I finished my last final for the semester, not knowing the news I would soon receive.

A few weeks later I received notification that due to not meeting the minimum GPA and missing it by 0.68 of a point, I would be suspended from school for the next semester. Tears fell from my eyes as I sat no longer feeling the weight of God's anointing, but instead the weight of failure. How could this happen? I worked so hard! What do I do now? Even though I was almost thirty years old, my next question sent my mind running, "How do I explain this to my mom? What do I tell my husband?" Tears turned to moans and moans turned to wails as I sat rocking, praying that this was not real and praying for some kind of relief; only to find none. This day was etched in my mind as the first nervous breakdown I experienced. In that moment, every word God spoke escaped me and I felt as if everyone that saw me, whether they knew me or not, knew that I had failed school. Despite the fact that I was invited to come back the following fall, all I could process was that, in that moment, it was over.

Christmas and New Years of 2008 to this day are a blur, but the days following my thirtieth birthday are crystal clear. Having just received the news of the school suspension, I felt like I was just catching my breath and I was just becoming able to see the sun shining and hear birds chirping again. As I was preparing for the spring semester of my dance studio, I received a letter stating that unless I could come up with $25,000 within the next seven days, I would have to leave. I later discovered that the amount demanded was due to something pending with the property, but since I was occupying the property, the debt had become mine. Crushed, my body sank to the floor, and again, the inexplicable presence of my tears arose. This time I had no voice, and I had no strength or will to push. One week later, I began packing. There were days that I packed in silence which proved to be the most tormenting ones. The days I played music, all I could imagine were the kids that should have been there but were not. I remember one day I was pulling down my curtains and a lady walked in. She had received my flier some months before and was coming to inquire about classes. As she walked in, she said, "Well hello! Are you redecorating?" I tried to muster up some kind of smile to greet her, but my sorrow would not allow it. In my reply, I advised her that I was not redecorating but instead moving out. She responded, "Oh wow, that was fast," and began laughing as she exited out the front door. I continued to weep as I pulled down my curtains, feeling as if I had been sentenced to watch this vision die with no ability to save it. I moved each piece out, primarily alone, piece by piece and day by day.

The night before the deadline, I paced the floor of my 3,500 square-foot studio. I touched every wall and mirror. I walked up to the doors, knowing that the property by that time was empty, but praying that someone with the ability to do so, would show up with the $25,000 I needed to keep my dream alive. I continued to pace and cry, praying for a miracle. I cannot place when it happened, but at some point, it did, where God led me to a place of worship. I found myself on the inside of the same door I often worshiped Him in front of before obtaining the space. As I hit my knees, the conversation went something like this:

Me: God what are you doing? Why are you allowing this?

Him: Are you sure you want to know?

Me: (Yelling) YES! I want to know! Why would You allow me to have this space and rip it from me in not only the same city I grew up in but in the same neighborhood, too?

Him: Because you praised Me when I gave it to you; I need to see your response if I take it. I need you to realize that even this building cannot hold you. This building will stay just like this until either you give it up or come back for it.

As I wept in the floor, the only feeling of consolation was to worship Him. Flashes of children flooded my mind along with the loss of my placement in school, but all I had in that moment were my tears in response. The worship became so intense that I became scared to even open my eyes. I was thinking that if I did, I would literally see the feet of Jesus. The weight and power of His presence flooded my soul; worship was my only resolve. Before leaving that night, and after locking the doors, I grabbed the door handles and said, "Stay right here, I will be right back."

For months following, it felt like a roller coaster. The next month, I graduated from a leadership program I was enrolled in that was hosted by my Pastor at the time. When March came, it greeted me with a letter advising that our house was headed into foreclosure. Crushed again, we found an agency that assisted with those types of situations only to find out that they could not help us. Four weeks later, I found myself again packing up my dreams, as we had to surrender the house we had built from the ground up. The day before the move, I was cleaning out the refrigerator in silence. All of a sudden, a weight hit me again, followed by weeping and screaming. When I came to myself, I awoke on the floor, soapy washcloth in hand and the light from the refrigerator door greeting me. I wanted to get up, but it seemed easier to just lay there. When I finally collected myself, I called someone to vent, but they advised they were too busy and would call back later. By May 2009, the marriage was over and in June 2009, I became a single mother. What made it even worse was that I no longer had a church home, as the hurt I had endured was just too much to stay there, serving in lay leadership and all. Within the same month, I reconnected with an old friend, who after getting the scoop on everything that had happened, told me that the best thing I could do was to go out with her. She told me that this would get me out of my funk, and yes, after trying what I called "everything else," I was convinced that this had to work.

For well over a year, I stayed in the club circuit weekend in and weekend out. I found that this was the place where I could tap into who I was way before all of the "hits" came and become someone I had never been. I remember being mean to men on purpose, because I was determined to use them the way I felt that I had been used. I remember partying all night, leaving drunk but still not being able to fill the broken places through alcohol and people.. I would work all week and party all weekend while my son was away. I would take the attention that men paid to me and try to find a place to use it to fill the cracks in my armor. When I saw people, I knew from 'church' I would quickly walk the other way. By this point, I knew the rumors that had been spread about me were too many to chase down and destroy. In the midst of my running from God, He always found me even when I was in the club.

I will never forget the moment when a man, dark in appearance motioned for me to come over in the club. I gave him my best walk; you know the one we practice in the mirror. With my dress and five-inch stilettos in tow, I approached him with a smile. He looked at me and said, "Why are you here with them? Who are they to you," as he referred to those, I came in the door with? I replied, "Oh those are my friends!" He responded, "No they're not. When they walked in, my homeboy and I had already decided what we would do to them, but when you entered, my tongue went to the roof of my mouth and didn't move until you walked over here. I don't know who you are or where you are supposed to be, but I need for you to get back there because you are messing up my high." Shocked and borderline offended, despite my faces and reply, his posture did not shift, not one time. Even in the dark places, as the Word states in Psalm 139, God was there. Even in my darkest places, God was still using me. One Sunday morning, I woke up; still dressed from the night before and with my shoes on that I was too drunk to remove, I opened my eyes. The sun was brighter than I had ever seen. Suddenly, I heard a loud, booming voice say, "Are you done yet? Can I be God now?" This voice was not unfamiliar to me, but it was unexpected, as I felt so far away and undeserving to hear God's voice. In that moment, I had no fight. I had lost what I deemed to be everything except my precious son who became my push to survive. I don't even remember crying this time. I only remember saying, "Yes God."

From that moment to this, God has been rebuilding. From my relationship with Him, to forgiving my former husband

and having the faith to believe and dream again. Brick after brick He has been rebuilding me. The loss was public, and left many assuming the worst of me, only for God to resurrect and restore the best in me. For years, I kept my head down and my dreams at bay, never believing in God's ability to restore me. This brings truth to power, as God took the remnants of my broken soul to restore publicly even in the midst of those who almost watched me die publicly. God has restored my ability to dream and pursue. Back then, I did not know that church hurt was necessary to make me a better Pastor, but it has. I did not know that closing a dance studio would pave the way to open many other businesses in confidence, but it did. I did not anticipate watching my son become the amazing young man he is today or being the vessel that God would use to birth our baby girl into the world, but God did it. I never imagined that God would send someone into my life, in the form of my husband, who understood where I had been and was willing to love me through it and help push me into my BEST place, but He has. I did not know that all these experiences and more would birth a warrior in me. One who would be willing and determined to declare the win from the front, but God did it, and I am so grateful for it. I am so grateful for it.

CHAPTER 5

"OUT OF BONDAGE"

BY CAROLYN RICE-SMITH

Ecclesiastes 3:1 (KJV) "
To everything there is a season, and a time
to every purpose under Heaven.

Wow, what a powerful reading that speaks to time and purpose. But first let me ask a question, have you ever felt like you were in too deep, was there too long, or that there was no hope?

Well, allow me to help you, there is hope! There is no time, no distance or limitations when it comes to God and there is nothing too hard for Him. There's a song that says, "If he has to reach way down, Jesus will pick you up!" But let me say it this way, Jesus will pick you out and up!

Bondage: Is the condition of not being free because you are strongly influenced by something or someone. (Thesaurus Collins Dictionary)

Out: moving or appearing to move away from a particular place especially one that is enclosed or hidden. (Dictionary.com)

"Out of bondage" is my story but just maybe it'll cause you to identify bondage within yourself or someone you know. But guess what? Stuck is stuck. Deception is deception, and bondage is bondage. Bondage doesn't have to be in the same form, but destruction is always written over it. Bondage, whether it's what you are aware of or if you are blind to it, the enemy's tactic doesn't change. It is to steal, kill and destroy. However, most importantly, it is possible to find a way out. In the beginning, middle, or at the end of the day, the intent of my story is to cause truth to be revealed and to bring hope to the hopeless, light to the darkness and freedom to those who are bound!

My bondage was drug addiction. Oh, but God! Let me take a moment and encourage somebody. Don't give up on yourself, a loved one or maybe even a friend. Maybe it has been a long journey, maybe even a rough one that feels impossible to get out of. But I'm living proof that deliverance can happen.

Can I give you hope? How about a nugget? Love and prayer unconditionally are power to the soul. It will break chains. It is a weapon against the enemy. You must have somebody that will love you enough to war with you and for you, no matter what. They must stand in the gap in spite of, because there is an enemy after our soul that will point out every truth, disappointment and act of wrong, to make you throw in the towel. The enemy wants to have his way and cause total destruction. There are benefits in having someone to fight on your behalf until breakthrough happens!

Living through the chains...was the truth of the matter.

Drugs

I did it, enjoyed it, wanted it, lived a long time in it, and yet was blinded to it! The enemy is so cunning and deceptive, no matter what form or bondage he comes in. It's our mindsets that tell us, "It's not that bad, we can stop when we are ready. It's a mindset that tells us it's not that bad, we can't stop or it's really not hurting anything." This is the enemy's voice of deception. Bondage is a thief that never intends to let go and will never allow you to become your best self or be in control. It will have you being a slave to destruction at the expense of your greatness. I was targeted by the enemy before I ever discovered me. Experiencing pain and rejection was truly no stranger to me. Rejected by a father but smiling through the pain and experiencing motherhood at a very early age. Being addicted to drugs became a way of life all while not realizing the depth of its destruction. I was not realizing how much pain it was causing, or even just how much I missed out on by not being involved in a lot of things. As I sit in a space now and look back, I can see the light of being out of bondage and also see the dark places that the enemy desired to take me out through the lies, tricks and plots of destruction that I couldn't see then. I now expose those same things to all that will receive. When it's all said and done, we wonder sometimes, "Why did I do this and that?" Why did I go through this and that?" I say it serves as a testimony to our sovereign God and his being and also to expose the enemy's plot of destruction. I speak hope, truth, and deliverance to other individuals that may be bound.

Transparency Is the Key to Deliverance

The story of "Out of Bondage" has much more to it like what gives the enemy access to draw us into places, experiences, and encounters of bondage that affect our thoughts, emotions, and perceptions. This is just a preview of what "Out of Bondage" is all about.

Take a look at what's next...

The Wake-Up Call....Once was Blind but Now I See

The moment came that then revealed I had failed at what I thought I had been protecting in all the years of my addiction. I was devastated...broken beyond measure. This was the turning point that began to open my eyes. My heart was then compacted with pain and love all at once. The desire to be delivered was so intense that heaven got the news!

When time meets time... some things are going to happen.

Galatians 4:4 (NIV), "But when the set time had fully come."

It was time to walk out of the bondage. It had held me captive for 20 years. It was a conversation that God strategically provoked that led me to the light of Truth. And it hurt so bad that the tears wouldn't stop falling. It was in that moment that I have vowed that I would not take another generation to what I had taken them through. Love was my driving force; it was then that I could begin to feel. Thank you all for never giving up on me and you, dear Mama, I know you prayed a many prayers though you didn't get a chance to witness the manifestation of my deliverance; but, it happened! Love you, Mama. You see, people counted me out, but the truth of the matter is this, some would have rather said, "That's where I would have always been (bound)." More to the point though, it was God's plan that freedom belongs to me. Those were some dark days in my life -- what I was calling good times (high). That was the furthest from the truth. There were a lot of times getting high was taking place. But also, during those times, talking about God and listening to gospel music is what we did. Proverbs 3:6, the King James version says, acknowledge Him in all thy ways...this is what we did. For me, even though I knew what I was doing wasn't right, I felt like a part of me still had to connect to God. I believed something good was happening because of it and that the enemy (Satan) was not getting all acknowledgement because getting high was taking place. All was not bad, all the time. There were highlights in my life. One of those things being, I loved writing poetry. I would like to share one of those poems I wrote. Also, I would like to say, don't ever stop dreaming. Sometimes times may be dark in the moment, but God can turn it around. I wrote this poem and it was one that won entry into publication. This poem is titled Dreams.

A Long Way From home, where things seem unfamiliar;

Because a trap in time, set out to steal ya.

Where smoke rises, and where even dreams get lost;

Into thin air, where the winds blow and toss.

It's never too late, to make Known the unknown;

To put a face on a dream so it can be shown.

To resurrect a dream, that got lost in the past;

Then this contest came along, and I thought here's my chance.

From this talent I write, from which there's more;

Now today I give wings, and God's blessings now soar.

When God Changes our Story

You see, my life didn't change in the moment of writing that poem. What I am saying, is God did do it! I am now at a time in my life where Out of Bondage is my reality! All I can say is Wow! When God turns it and does a new thing, freedom takes place!!!

CHAPTER 6

CENTER STAGE

BY TORREE MUNSON

Preparation for Center Stage

T here she is, sitting there all alone wanting and yearning to be loved. She needs to feel loved, but she looks for it in all the wrong places. She needs just someone to listen to her, to hear what she has to say. Oh, she has so much bottled up inside of her that it has taken root in her spirit; but she doesn't know that. She just wants some answers. She has many questions. For her, where are the answers?

She is a grown woman, but deep inside there is a little girl curled up within really scared to live. Scared to take the "bull by the horns" to step out into her destiny and fulfill her mandate that God has for her. But what she fails to realize or know is that God created her for greatness. He has placed a lioness spirit in her. She does not "stand down." She goes to get everything that God has for her. She is scared of nothing and she protects everything that is connected to her. Unfortunately, she doesn't know this yet because the little girl is still trapped inside of her. But she believed the God that answers by fire.

She lays down in deep thought, wondering will she ever see herself in a better place. Will she ever have the guts to do what God has called her to do with all this baggage? Can she believe enough to start moving and get out of stagnation? She is dreaming and wanting more, but it continues to be a dream until she takes the initiative to get moving. All she does is cry and wonder, why me?

Step One: Transform your Mind

Now, let's see how to connect with the little girl that is scared of the spotlight. Who is she and how did she get here? Well, God created her in His image and in His likeness. She is a child of the King. She is the righteousness of Christ and she carries His DNA. DNA stands for Divine Nature Authority. But she doesn't realize that she has the authority of her Father to speak and to change the dynamics of her life, so she stays bound by her past.

She feels insecure at times because she feels like she is not good enough. She thinks everybody looks down on her and her self-esteem is low. Maybe her clothes are not as pretty as theirs, so she thinks. Her shoes are not the latest and the newest style that is out right now. Oh, her nails can never get done because right now she can't afford it. Let us not leave out the hair. She wears her hair pulled back in a ponytail all the time because she cannot afford those long weaves down to her butt, and she can't even afford a wash and set these days. This makes her feel like she is not in the game anymore. Everyone has one up on her and she cannot compete with the latest and the greatest. Now her self-esteem is low, and she does not even believe in herself. When she was younger, she was talked about, and had to fight to make it through. It seems as a child she had it very hard. Some may say she was spoiled, but they didn't know what she was feeling inside. Why? It was because things transitioned in her life that she couldn't stop. Things just happened. Now she is full grown, and she is still asking herself, why me? Why do I have to have a hard life? What did I do to deserve this? Why is my body stricken with pain? Why do I feel all alone sometimes? She feels like things will never get better.

I must say, no one is exempt from anything in life. So, the key here is how we look at the situation. In order for us to move past all that God allowed the enemy to present to us, we must then take charge of our thought process.

The Word of God states, in Romans 12:2, "And be not conformed to this world: but be ye transformed by the renewing of your mind, that ye may prove what is that good, and acceptable, and perfect, will of God." The Word also says in Philippians 2:5, "Let this mind be in you, which was also in Christ Jesus."

What is the Bible saying? God is telling us not to think like this world. Don't give in to the world. You are the righteousness of Christ. You have to condition yourself to change your thought process. See, you can't say what your brain won't do or how your brain thinks or what the brain won't allow you to do. You have to allow your mind to be transformed, which is spiritual, as the Word of God says. Let this mind be in you which was also in Christ Jesus. That's the word!!!! It takes time, yes, you have to keep speaking it into existence.

This is called FAITH. The word says in Hebrews 11:1, "Now faith is the substance of things hoped for, the evidence of things not seen." You must have faith to see things happen in the spiritual realm before it manifests in the natural. You need the faith to bring it to pass. Stop thinking negative concerning yourself. That thought process is not God. That thought comes from your enemy which is the father of all lies and his name is Satan. So, you can't accept these thoughts when they come into your mind, you have to cast it down and speak life to every situation that seems too hard or impossible.

Call on your Father, He states in His Word, Isaiah 54:10, "No weapon that is formed against thee shall prosper; and every tongue that shall rise against thee in judgment thou shalt condemn. This is the heritage of the servants of the LORD, and their righteousness is of me, saith the LORD."

He said it. Listen, nothing that the enemy throws at you will prosper. You have to believe it. See, God is His Word, and His Word is Him. He is not a man that He shall lie. Now, this is your time and season to forget those things of the past; let the baggage go, get rid of it. Drop the load off at your Father's doorstep and tell Him to take it. You have to learn to pick your battles; every battle is not for you to fight. Trust God. You have to learn to trust Him. You have tried it your way and it does not work. It is time to put it in the Master's hand. He is ready to create the MASTERPIECE, which is you. So, now wipe your tears and get your mind right. If you need a couple more days take them. However, once you have cried it all out, it is time to get ready for your next step. The next step may be hard and too difficult for some but is necessary for you in order to move forward and walk into your destiny.

I had to really overcome some things in my life in order to move forward. I had to find that little girl so that I could get to the root of the issue for me. I wanted to be whole and I wanted to be free from the hurt and pain that I was feeling. I was ready for change and deliverance to take place in my life. I had to cry out to God to help me make this change in my life that ultimately could leave me stagnated if I decided not to change or propel me forward if I wanted to change. Remember, it's a choice to stay stuck or to move. Which decision will you make today? It is time to choose because the Center Stage is waiting on you.

Preparation for Center Stage

She is not ready because she holds the clothes sitting in the dressing room with tears in her eyes. She is struggling and fighting at the same time to get herself together. She tells herself she can, but she doesn't really believe it because of the pain that has crippled her. She just doesn't know how to take that next step. It hurts so bad; doubt and fear rippled through her.

Step 2: Forgiveness

This is a step that you cannot afford to not carry out because this is called baggage as well. This baggage can most definitely cause sickness in your body. We must learn to forgive. Now forgiving is going to give you peace but I must say it is not easy to do. It takes God for this. You will definitely need His strength because this one, oh, you can't do this alone. You will need supernatural strength and power to help you overcome those that have hurt you, abused you, misused you, lied on you, tried to mess up your name, and the list goes on. But it is MANDATORY; you must do this to allow yourself to be free from church people and non-church people. It doesn't matter because hurt is hurt. Yet it seems when you are hurt by church people it tends to hit in a different way. I guess because we believe that they should know better, and they should not behave as the world. Well, it's time to wake up and smell the coffee because all people in church aren't right and the fact of the matter is that God has given us gifts without repentance. This means individuals can act church in church and become another individual outside of church. Some believe that they are exempt from the wrath of God and they have arrived because the enemy has them blinded. When it is all said and done, you need to ask God to help you forgive.

I had to ask God to help me forgive my ex-husband for the infidelity, the STD he gave me, the mental and physical abuse and just making me feel uncomfortable. I felt like I was walking on eggshells in my house. Oh, yeah, when it was bad -- it was bad, and when it was good, I was happy. I asked the Father, Lord, please get me out of this marriage. This is torture for me to live like this. I am not happy, and I am becoming depressed. I began to feel suicidal and almost had a nervous breakdown. I called my girlfriend and I told her that I thought I was having a nervous breakdown. I heard voices. I felt like I was out of it all the time. I don't even know how I came out of it at all. All I know is that I was miserable. We were Pastors and I could not believe that this was my life. Whoa, I was in a state of shock that I was literally going through a death walk in my life. I was really struggling. We eventually got separated and I turned into another person. I started drinking and became another individual that I didn't even know. I was happy doing it. I was living in sin because I was so hurt and torn. Yes, it was going to take the blood of Jesus to get me out of this one.

As time went on, I eventually came out of this lifestyle and forgave him with God's help. I really began to feel sorry for him and began to pray for him. The more I prayed, God began to deal with my spirit more and more to extend compassion for him. He eventually apologized and the relationship was healed for the sake of our daughter. Now, a year has passed, and it is like nothing has ever happened, but this is because I let it go and I forgave him. No, I did not want to stay mad at him forever. I did not want to live with anger in me. I wanted to be free and move on not allowing him to have control over me.

I will say that he had past hurt issues that he never dealt with and this was one of the reasons I went through what I went through with him. He was hurt and torn as well. This is an example of individuals not being healed and how it can ripple to another individual and continue to keep causing hurt and pain. This will continue to be a cycle until individuals seek healing and deliverance. The enemy wants to continue to cause havoc in the lives of the people of God, so they will not progress! I speak life to every situation in your life and peace in your mind. You will not die, you shall live!

Preparation for The Stage

Putting on her shoes, she takes a deep breath and prepares for center stage. The hardest part was letting go of the unforgiveness that kept her holding the clothes in her hand. As she walks up to the mirror, she holds the clothes up to herself and imagines herself in the clothes and her feet in the heels feeling and looking like new money. Yet she just couldn't put them on. But after this visual, baby, she is starting to feel her help and strength coming. She is preparing.

Step 3: Discovering ME

I have forgiven and released people out of my life and have moved on to a better me. I was finding my purpose in life; no longer allowing the issues that hurt me to hinder me anymore. I was doing the spiritual work that was needed to continue to strengthen my walk in Christ. When you have been hurt and severely damaged in your spirit like I had, when you do get delivered, you've got to press into God at all cost. I found myself praying more and seeking righteous things more. I fasted; I studied the Word more. If you have ever been hurt at the measure that I was hurt, then you know this is a hard resolve to come to. But when you do, you recognize God still has a plan and purpose for your life. Inside of you is greatness...no matter what you have gone through or done. So I encourage you as well to increase your prayer time with the Father. Miss a couple of meals; fasting is always good for your spirit. Dive deep into the Word of God, so , you can hear Him as He speaks to you. You don't want your flesh to get in the way of you hearing what the Father is telling you to do. You want to make sure that your spirit is sensitive to the Father. This means that you will have to shut the TV off sometimes. Give up your favorite show for the favorite One in your life. Take a break from them and allow God to minister to you one on one. Be still, sit in pure silence and allow God's voice to ring in your ears with what He wants you to do. Let him direct you how He wants you to move and flow. See, the Lord is very strategic in his ways and what He has planned for you.

The Word of God says in Jeremiah 29:11 (NIV), "For I know the plans I have for you, "declares the Lord, "plans to prosper you and not to harm you, plans to give you hope and a future."

I want you to understand that you will always go through something, but it is the way you look at the situation. I remember when God began to deal with me with my purpose, there was a test that I had to go through to get to it. God had to refine, sharpen, and purify me for the greater that was coming in my life. You see, if you seek Him you will find Him.

The Word of God says in Jeremiah 29:13 (KJV), "And you will seek Me and find Me, when you search for Me with all your heart."

God is waiting on you to search for Him. He is waiting on you to seek Him so that He can reveal to you your purpose. He wants you to walk in your purpose and get everything that He has for you. It is all up to you -- the ball is in your court.

The Word of God says in 1 Peter 1:7 (AMP), "So that the genuineness of your faith, which is much more precious than gold which is perishable, even though tested and purified by fire, may be found to result in your praise and glory and honor at the revelation of Jesus Christ."

Listen, all the tests that I have endured to be where I am today was so that God can position me for greatness. I have learned so much about me. I have grown, and I know who I am because I sought the face of Jesus! I was hungry for Him. I wanted to know who I was and when I got in the face of the king, He revealed this and more to me. I am stronger, wiser, and I am a King's kid! So, I walk with authority and power from my Father.

I know that if you want out of the pain and hurt, you can get out. Begin to seek the Father and allow Him to reveal who you are and His purpose for you.

Approaching Center Stage

The strength that she has now, whew, she would have never imagined in a million years. After applying her make-up, she put on her clothes, stepped into her PINK STILLETOS, combed her hair out while repeating to herself that she is the righteousness of Christ. She takes a deep breath and opened the door. She walks toward backstage slowly in her stiletto pumps telling her Father thank you. Now, she is positioned right on the marker, and she is ready, no doubts or fears. The announcement is made, the curtains fly open, and she steps out to the center stage. The crowd cheers her on. The smile she has on her face represents the love that God has shown towards her -- the power that God has given her to face adversity and pain. She doesn't look like what she has been through because God was covering her the whole time.

Stage 4: Dream Again

When God turned the captivity of Zion, they were ones that dreamed again according to Psalm 126:1. Because I pressed pass my pain, forgave, and turned my life back over to God, I am now free to dream again. I am never looking back, and sister, I encourage you to do the same. Your past can either be a prison for you or the fuel you need to embrace the prophetic destiny that God has for you. Hopefully, you will choose the latter; one decision can change your life for the better.

CHAPTER 7

THE BLESSINGS
IN THE MOVES!

BY STACEY MASSEY LOGAN

A lot of times we second guess what we hear God tell us to do and when He says to do it. It is sad to say, but some of us have been so programmed to only hear God through other people that when He speaks to us directly, we second guess it. Because of this, we do not move and when we tell people that we heard God say this or that, they try to downplay it and make you feel like you didn't hear God. But I thank God for the Spirit of Obedience!!! Glorrrr-ry!!! Hallelujah!!

In 2003, I moved back to my hometown because I was being told I needed to come home. My dad was getting older and his memory was not the same, so I needed to be closer. I prayed, and I moved back with my family to my hometown to be closer to my dad and other family members. Believe me, when I tell you that obedience is key. When God says something in your NOW, it definitely affects your FUTURE. Glorr-ry!!! Sorry, I keep getting excited about where this chapter is going. I have known the call on my life for a long time. Oh, did I tell you, I was a preacher's kid? So, you know some of us run from the call. However, when God says, "STOP," oh, the blessings that come with the stop. In my move back home, God only allowed me to pack what I could fit in my car. I was like, "What Lord?" There was no moving truck. He told me to give up all my stuff. "Are you serious?? Lord, sell all my stuff and only take what will fit in my car and trunk?" I cried and cried, "Lord, I worked too hard to get all the things I have, and I have to sell it." God said to me, "I allowed you to have those things. Sell them and trust me." Even in selling all the stuff that God had blessed us with, I still had a question for God. Where are we supposed to live? He said, "I got this. Just be obedient." Two days later my dad called me to tell me that my former pastor's daughter was willing to rent to me her father's house because he had passed a few years prior and it was empty. Look at God! Rent was reasonable and it was close to most of the important places we would need to go. After struggling with selling my stuff even after he opened the door to housing for us, I packed up the car with enough space for the family and back to Illinois from Tennessee we went. The truth was this, I loved being in Tennessee, but I had experienced so much mental, physical, emotional, spiritual, self-inflicted, involuntary hurt that honestly, if I would have stayed, I may not be here today to write this chapter for you. BUT GOD!

We finally reached our new home, which I thanked God for. It was not what I expected because it had been empty for some years and needed some work., Yet if you know me you know I'm Ms. Handy Dandy. As we were getting settled in and fixing stuff the way we wanted it and praying and anointing it, God said, "This is a pass-through house to get you to where you are going." When He said this, it was August 2003. Let me tell you how He worked everything out. Did I mention, I had three children and was going through a divorce? But God! By October, He had blessed me with a job making decent money for 2003. I still had a car, every bit of furniture and some we had sold. We had it back. Spiritually, I began to grow again. My divorce was almost final. I could keep naming blessings. Most of all, I was back home to be able to hear my daddy preach, "Them Dry Bones, Can They Live," and hear him put his famous twist on the Lord's Prayer on Sunday mornings when we sung it. Everything seemed to be going well and you know the enemy started getting upset because I didn't die in my depression and hurt when I tried to commit suicide. That is another story for another book. But God! In January of 2005, God told me to apply for Section 8 housing assistance. I didn't know why, but I did. Let me tell you God will set you up for a blessing. Be obedient! Around March of 2005, strange things started happening in the house (spiritually), and then it physically started falling apart. No matter how much we prayed against the spirits that were attacking us in the house and fixed the stuff that was going on with the actual house, God had another plan. We had to have some major work done to the house, which required an inspector. The workers came to give us an estimate on the work and the inspector was there too. Well, the inspector slapped a big "UNINHABITABLE DWELLING" on the front door. "Do you mean we can't live here?" "Ma'am, this property is NOT safe for you and your children. You have 45 days to move." It was all making sense why God had me to go to the Housing Authority to complete an application for public housing and Section 8. If you know anything about the difference between the two, one is moveable and the other one is not. He gave me a letter to take to the housing authority to show that they were condemning our house to see if they could assist us with housing. Believe me when I tell you that God showed us FAVOR. We got accepted and approved for Section 8, and were able to find a 3-bedroom townhouse and moving assistance within the 45 days. But God! We moved in, got settled, and we had more space than before. My daughter had her space, my two sons shared a space, and I had a space. We had a blast. I still was growing spiritually, but then I backslid. (SMH – Shaking my Head). I still went to church, did everything I was supposed to, but my partying etc. was causing me to slide back into familiar and unknown territory. I never stopped going to church or praying, praising, worshiping, but God was not pleased. Even though He allowed me to accomplish some things, He still was not pleased with my actions. From 2006 to 2009, He moved me four times. He allowed me to lose a set of twins that almost killed me. He allowed me to pay off two cars and a truck, but I still lost them for one reason or another. The last move, He gave us a purple mini-van and a house around the corner from the church. You may know that the #4 is the number of seasons. It was my season and I hadn't even realized it. Even though I had straightened up and was back on the path for 2009-2011, I still had some things I was battling, but I was winning. It wasn't the streets; it was depression and rejection, which I later realized these were triggers for my downward spiral. I knew God had a greater call on my life other than the ministry I was doing at church. Even though I was allowed to work in several aspects of ministry, I didn't feel like I was doing enough for what God had shown me. God was calling me to do more. I told my leaders what I heard God say to me so many times, but due to my past it stopped them from moving me forward in ministry. Also, I was told that God didn't tell them that. In June 2010, my dad started getting worse. "Lord, you gotta help me because I was a daddy's girl." My daddy walked in the hospital July 2010, on a Saturday afternoon, by that Monday, he could not walk. I watched the man that had poured God into my life and taught me about having a personal relationship with him, slowly leaving me. God knew my daddy was the main reason I moved back to Illinois. "Lord, if you want me to stay here, you gotta keep my daddy here." Sad to say, my daddy left me August 14, 2010. Noooo, we had so many more years of studying the Bible together, writing sermons, baseball, traveling, etc. I knew that my daddy had passed the mantle to me a few days after he passed. He came to me in my dream and gave instructions and to tell me, he was proud of me and no matter how sad I was, hear God's voice in everything.

In November 2010, I was introduced to my cousin from Brooklyn, New York. He was Bishop-Designate at the time. When we met, there was a pulling in the spirit, and I didn't understand what it was until a few months later. He invited the kids and I to come to his consecration service in Indianapolis, IN, the weekend of April 1, 2011. Watch how fast God moves in this next move. But God! We went to the consecration and God spoke to me and said, "Pack, you are going to New York." I said, "NOPE, who wants to be in New York?" God said it again, "Pack, you are going to New York to help him build and restructure the ministry and to cover him." I said, "Lord, he's a Bishop, how am I supposed to cover him and help him restructure the church" He said, "I have already put in you what is needed." I was like, "Yeah, right, I'm not going to New York." That Tuesday morning God said, "Get up and go put in your housing transfer to New York." I laid there like..."Uh, nope, sorry can't do that one," until He said it again with a little more authority. I got up and went and got the paperwork for the transfer. Yet the whole time I was still saying, "I'm not going to New York. Who's got money for New York?" I was grumbling and complaining, but still being obedient. That night, God had me call my cousin just to check in and see how he was doing. I abruptly spoke out of my mouth. God had me say, "I'm coming to New York to help you restructure and build the ministry." I did not know he had been praying for Help! He said, "Do what...when?" He finally composed himself. I said God said, "I have to come and help you restructure and rebuild the church." At this point, I still don't know how my two sons and I and all of our stuff were supposed to get to New York. After talking to my cousin, the Bishop, I did the rest of the leg work to turn in the portability paperwork. I was still telling the Lord, "I really don't see this happening." Once the paperwork was in, there was no turning back. I finally got the okay to tell the leaders that I was serving under that I was going to New York with my cousin to help him at his church. The response was one that, I will not put in this story. But it is definitely in the upcoming book. Needless to say, once again God said, "Give EVERYTHING away, but what you can fit in your suitcase." "WHAT GOD?!!!!! I have less than the last time I had to give away everything." I started praying even harder, "Lord, we don't have tickets. I have to meet the new landlord by this date. I must be in New York by this date for a briefing. There was so much that was going through my head. Remember, I did my transfer request around April 4, 2011, we were in New York by May 27, 2011.

Long story short, the move wasn't just for my cousin/Bishop, it was for me. So many of the ministry gifts and talents that I had suppressed and hid because they were not being used at home, all began to bloom, blossom, grow, and manifest. I felt like a garden that had been dry and got some fresh water. Not to say that I was not growing where I was, but not the way God needed me too. God allowed me to go through the steps of an Evangelist, to become an Adjutant, to Minister, and now to be an Elder with an Outreach Ministry in Atlanta, GA.

There was one last move of giving up EVERYTHING to follow God's instructions and that is where I am now in Atlanta, GA, where God has allowed me to be the founder of HBOM- Highways & Byways Outreach Ministry ATL. One of the Founding Members of Chozen Diamonds ATL., and the CEO & Founder of THTC. This is not even my end there is so much more to come.

There was a BIGGER BLESSING in each move. Who would have thought when this chapter started, I would end up here! Moral of the chapter - Do not let your past define your future, let it push you into your future! Hear God for yourself and be obedient even when you don't understand! He is Faithful to HIS WORD!

Thank You for Reading. I hope this Blessed you!

CHAPTER 8

LET GO TO WALK INTO YOUR PURPOSE

BY IRIS CARR

I am a divorced mother of three beautiful children. I always dreamed of having an amazing family with children. I didn't think I would go through a divorce or any other hardship in life. I dreamed of traveling and speaking on behalf of marriages, relationships and families. I remembered a prophecy that I was told many times, "My marriage is going to get worse before it gets better, and it was up to me." I do believe God allows things to perform a work on us -- to strength our spiritual maturity. Even though I wanted things from the Lord, I had some issues within me that needed to be dealt with. I had to get to the root cause of my issues before I could walk into my destiny. I had to acknowledge and recognize who I am. It does not matter where I was born, but it matters how my thoughts processed me into who I am in Christ.

During my childhood, I witnessed my mother's divorce and mental challenges before she transitioned to the other side of the world. As I reflect, I didn't understand why she was going through this. As a child, the picture was painted as is. She was having a rough time in her marriage and her relationship with family members that affected her in many areas of her life. I didn't understand as a child, but when I began to live my life, I went through many similar struggles. I would tell myself, I will not end up like my mother, but not knowing the root cause -- the same happened to me.

The enemy tried to attack the very thing I dreamed and had passion for. He tried to destroy who I am in Christ. He was trying to take my identity and my mind. He had plans to distract me, but God had a plan. I felt like there was no hope for me. I felt like I didn't have a purpose because of my failure. I was confused and felt at times, the devil had my mind. I thought I was losing both my mind and everything around me. The devil knew my purpose and he had a plan to destroy me. He plotted seeds of lies during my childhood concerning my mother and family. And now years later, I went through a separation, divorce, and my name being scandalized and lied on. It was a pattern of what my mother had gone through.

Going through a divorce in my last pregnancy was complicated. I was alone in the hospital. I had no one to comfort or console me. During that moment, I thought it was the end the world. I couldn't think of anyone but my mother. I realized then how much I missed her. The enemy tried to play with my mind once again. "You don't have a mother," "You're going to have it hard." "You can't raise the children by yourself." "You don't have anybody." I imagined everyone with their mothers and friends, and here I was alone. The mind is a terrible thing to waste. The enemy tried to attack my mind first. So, I turned it around. The enemy slowly plans to get into our minds. Whatever we think on long enough, we will eventually act on it. I discovered that if we begin to look at life in a negative way, it causes us to look at others, most of the time, in a negative way. This negative thinking is strong enough to change our moods; which cause problems in our health, relationships, and minds. It causes us to be emotional, but we have the authority to set the atmosphere. Negative thinking and actions bring about bad spirits that are not pleasing to the eyes of God. The more negative we think, the more it attracts negativity, and the more we keep ourselves in bondage. Even when most of our loved ones, close friends, and our enemies hurt us, we should forgive and release positive vibes. Yes, it could be hard to be encouraging and forgiving, but it all starts in our mind. It starts with renewing the mind. It is to help the mind, body, and soul. The more we exercise our minds with positive thoughts and words of inspiration, the better we become at it.

The devil may have meant it for bad, but it turned out for my good. When my mother passed, I didn't shed a lot of tears, but I did cry during lonely time I believe I was in a state of shock for years, but later it was a healing time for me. I thought I had lost my mind, but God; the Holy Spirit was within, comforting me. God, the Creator, sees more than our mistakes; so why focus on failure? You have a future; your destiny is ahead of you. Your past experience is what helps you see the light. The enemy will have us thinking negatively of ourselves so much that we begin planting corrupt seeds.

I noticed the women God put in my path as if He wanted me to pay attention to what He was doing, rather being distracted by the pain, and hurt of my childhood and family members. I realized also; I was growing spiritually. The Lord was getting my attention in what He placed on the inside of me.

Yet the negativity was distracting me. There was a time I did not know what my purpose was in life. I thought many things, but when I sought God and asked what my purpose was, He revealed part of my purpose throughout the course of my life. I have many talents and gifts that I did not acknowledge until later in my spiritual growth. My purpose lies in what I am passionate about. I found my passion through tests, trials, tribulation. I believe our talents and gifts help enhance our purpose.

We are going to make mistakes that we regret. It is okay because you can get back up again, and your Father in Heaven sees you more than your mistakes. Whatever we think of it, we will act on it. A person may not know he/she is acting out until she/he is acting out. Even then that person may feel bad about how they reacted. Negatives bring about different emotions such as anger, frustration, bitterness or fear. Often times our emotions will cause us to wander and become self-centered and selfish. Often when a person does someone harm, we call him/her our enemy, and there are other times we assume others may be against us because of what we may discern. If someone did another person wrong, then we should check and examine ourselves to forgive because it is only ourselves we will be hurting and not the other person. We have the power to speak over our lives as well as the individual who may have done the person harm. God may be using you to deliver this person from whatever they may be going through. And the person may not be aware of their actions.

I did not realize how scared I was until I stepped out of my comfort zone. I did enough to get by not knowing I had more within myself. Basically, I limited myself. I feared the unknown, but I knew there was more within me and was eager to grow. I felt like I was at the end of a dark tunnel. I could not do anything but look up and throw my hands up. I felt so alone that I had no other choice but to surrender. I understand now why it is important to surround yourself with positive people who are growing around you. I contemplated on what I had lost, and at times, I felt like I had lost everything. I can imagine how Job felt, but one thing I learned from Job, he did not give up on God. Yes, he was emotional, and he expressed himself, but he did not deny God. Throughout my experience, I realize at this point, it has developed me to see much clearly by giving me an understanding of life. In other words, I have gained wisdom.

Most of our memories and issues of life can distract us from making wise decisions but can also make and lead us in the direction of fulfilling our purpose. We become distracted concerning hardship in most areas of our lives. This includes marriage, relationships, jobs, families, finances, health, etc. and not solving the root cause of the problem or mental breakdown. It is important that we acknowledge and get an understanding of who we are. "For I know the plans I have for you," declares the Lord, "plans to prosper you and not to harm you, plans to give you hope and a future." We were created by an all-knowing God, who reigns and is the author and the finisher of all. No matter what we go through in life, we can get back up again because our Father, the Creator, wants us to prosper. We have the power to take authority to speak over our lives. We can break the patterns of our generation by having a positive attitude; having positive strategies; action; and most of all, relying on the Holy Spirit. I have learned that we gain spiritually and physically in the hard places in life if we depend and allow the Holy Spirit to guide the way. We are able to see differently and become wise. "My brethren, count it all joy when ye fall into divers temptations" (James 1:2). We are not exempt from our trials and tribulations. We are going to go through hard, dark, and complicated struggles in life. It is having the right attitude and the action that determines what we go through. We should know that God is there for us and He will not put more on us then we can bear.

So rejoice, because something good can come out of this, if we keep the right attitude.

I was not expecting a divorce or struggle while in poverty. But because of decisions I made, I had to suffer the consequences. I am not perfect, but I thank God for giving me a second chance, by His grace. If He can do it for me, I know I can forgive myself and others. I understand when I walk in forgiveness that things are working in my favor, spiritually and physically. I have been labeled, and yes, it hurts, but I had to learn to forgive. I had to learn to know when to speak and know when to be quiet. I have lost everything I had, but by the grace of God, I have my mind, and in reality, I have gained physically and spiritually. What you are going through is to make you strong. It is to make you and allow your eyes to come open to the things of the Spirit, so that you may be able to help others in wisdom and godly counseling. It is for someone else to witness and minister to and encourage. God allows things to happen because He trusts you. What you are going through is a process of what God is manifesting. Are you going to trust the process? Forgive, let go, and go through it! God gave His only Son, because of His love for His people that we may be forgiven to live spiritually free. His love for us is unconditional and if we receive Him, as our Father, and Savior and have faith in who He is, He will provide. I believe if we know and trust our Father, we will know who we are in Christ. There is a purpose for our lives, and this is the reason why our Heavenly Father loves us unconditionally. He knows the plans He has for our lives; plans to prosper and to give us hope. Who would ever think having the dreams of your life would be a process? No one imagined going through trials or tragedy to experience peace and joy. No one imagined their life to be a process of a product of their dream. We must be broken and go through some things in order to know what love is. We have to go through hardship in order to appreciate and enjoy life. The good news is this, we can enjoy life to the fullest by accepting and receiving the Holy Spirit, Jesus

Christ, as our Lord and Savior. You can accept Him where you are by believing He died on the cross for you. And, yes, He rose with all power in His hands, and we can have a relationship with Him. Let go, so you can walk in your purpose!

CHAPTER 9

SUPERBOWL SUNDAY 2015:
MY PINK STILETTOS

BY CARMEN A. SMITH

My journey to living life in its fullness didn't start until I was 47 years old. I grew up in church under the loving guidance of my mother, Delores Jean and my paternal grandparents, LC and Charles Etta. I knew God through their life experiences and teachings but didn't have a relationship with Him for myself. I foolishly and pridefully told myself over the years that I knew Him, but I only granted Him access to my life when it was convenient for me. I came to realize I was living off their prayers and God's grace and mercy towards me.

When I woke up on February 1, 2015, I recall having two things on my mind: going to church and more importantly, attending my friends' Superbowl party later that evening. I'm not your typical football fan. I only watch for the commercials and to socialize. Since I consider myself a chicken wing and martini kinda girl...well at least, I did, so attending a Superbowl party was going to be the highlight of my day. I was probably looking forward to the martinis, shaken not stirred, more than going to church. I knew going to church was the right thing to do. Remember, I was raised in church, so not going never seemed right. I attended church out of tradition and habit. I would experience feel good moments, but nothing lasting or fulfilling. Oftentimes when I left church, I felt guilty and depressed because I knew I needed more from God but didn't know how to get it. Every time I would hear the altar call, I allowed my heart to harden because I really didn't think I was that bad of a person. For many years, I refused to allow God into my life. Just imagine how depressing and conflicted I was feeling...most of my life. Church was supposed to be the place where you went for healing, hope and deliverance. I needed more than a good, hallelujah word from the preacher and uplifting songs. None of that was sustaining me. At some point, I needed an encounter with God that would completely and totally change my existence.

When I think back on that day, I don't even remember what the sermon was about or who preached. That sounds crazy to me because it was such a surreal day. One would think I should remember those details, but I really don't recall them. What I do remember, is feeling like my life was hopeless. I was constantly looking for happiness and peace, literally in all the wrong places and people. I was going through life aimlessly, day after day, no peace to be found and only momentary happiness. I believe I was a suicide waiting to happen. I could have been one of those people who committed suicide and people would say, "We didn't know she was so unhappy," or "I wish we said something because we saw the signs."

Thank God for His love, grace and mercy. He was watching over me even when I didn't recognize or choose Him. But this particular Sunday, Superbowl Sunday 2015, turned out to be the conduit to peace I was searching for all along.

Sitting up close in church wasn't to my liking. Being close to the Word or the preacher...looking at me made me feel uneasy. But for some reason, I decided to sit next to my cousin when she beckoned for me. Reluctantly, I moved from the back to the second row from the front...REALLY! After the sermon, the Pastor did what I literally HATED...He said, "turn to your neighbor, ask them if they have a personal relationship with the Lord and if they want to go up to the altar." This was too much! I couldn't look away and ignore my cousin, she was holding my hand and staring at me. That question always made me cringe deep inside. Although I felt angry, a defense mechanism, I guess, as tears were streaming down my face, my heart was softening. My cousin had one hand and one of the Elders had my other hand directing me to the altar. I felt like they were literally tossing me towards the feet of Jesus. They didn't move with me but the motion of their hands with mine drew me out the row towards the Savior. I still didn't have in my mind this was the day I would give my life to Christ. I just knew I was tired of merely existing and feeling lost and hopeless.

When the Elder at the altar asked, "What do you need?" all I could do was cry. However, when she asked again, I remember saying, "I want to be saved." She talked with me and then prayed the sinner's prayer with me. With a snotty nose and tears streaming down my face, I repeated those words of confession and repentance. It was like the Elder was reading my mind. She said, "You may not feel anything right now, but believe in your heart that God has forgiven you and you are saved." Before she spoke those words to me, I was thinking, "Is this it? I don't feel any different!" What I know now is the Holy Spirit was speaking to me, drowning out the doubt the enemy was trying to bring to my mind in that very moment. I was forgiven and cleansed of my sins and guess what; she was right! I left church with an assurance that I was forgiven of my sins. I still went to the Superbowl party, but I didn't drink. I felt such a wave of peace in my spirit. Nothing has ever compared to that feeling ever in my life. I wasn't worried about what people would think or how I was going to make it on this new journey. All I knew was that God had forgiven me and the peace I was experiencing had nothing to do with me, people or things. God heard my cry and prayers. Jesus became my Savior, and the Holy Spirit entered my heart and brought peace that surpasses my understanding, even to this day.

The living God of creation, the One my Mom and grandparents introduced to me as a child, had become a reality to me. These past five years walking with Christ have been full of peace, forgiveness, love, healing and revelation. God's Spirit is the only Spirit that can transform a life of hopelessness, despair and depression into something glorious for His benefit. I am His daughter and a beautiful masterpiece all because I said YES to His call upon my life. Life isn't all peaches and cream, but the grass is definitely greener and healthier on this side of the road. Holy Spirit lives inside my heart giving me the power and strength to continue living. I now aspire to let this newfound light shine through me, so others see God's hand in my life. Many layers of past hurts from dysfunctional relationships, low self-esteem and fragile self-confidence have been brought to the surface, resulting in my deliverance. God is always faithful to us. We are called to seek His face and worship Him. My desire to know God is deepened through prayer, worship and studying His Word. I have come to realize the Word of God is truly life-giving.. It sustains, strengthens, corrects and encourages me.

I was diagnosed with breast cancer six months after getting saved. God's grace brought me through, and I am thriving! I no longer suffer from depression due to the enormous grief I was experiencing after my Mother's death in 2008. I've had to acknowledge repressed feelings and memories from being molested as a young girl and never telling my family until 2017. Living day in and day out feeling as if I had no purpose and searching for love has come to an end. Living a life dedicated to Christ and seeking God for His plan for my life has given me purpose. I never dreamed I would become an author and minister in training, especially since I have struggled all my life with a fear of public speaking. Even when I was a kid reciting long Easter speeches my grandmother would choose for me, and dropping numerous public speaking classes in college, I didn't know God would use the very thing I struggled with to give me a voice and purpose to glorify Him.

God has shown me His love over and over. His love for me enables me to show Him love, to love myself and others. The love of God in my heart helps me to forgive God, myself and people. We cannot go through life harboring hatred and unforgiveness. It damages you internally and prevents you from experiencing the fullness of joy living for Christ. It is not easy allowing Holy Spirit to transform you...the flesh is truly used of the devil and doesn't want you to let go of hurt and rejection. But I often remind myself of the scriptures, "He who is in you is greater than he who is in the world" (I John 4:4) and "I can do all things through Christ who strengthens me." (Philippians 4:13). Whatever God has called me to do or reveals in me, He has equipped me to be an overcomer. As my spiritual Mom says, "That's good news to me."

From my blog, No Suga Coated Word Ministry:
"Mirror Mirror"

There was a time I looked in the mirror and didn't like what I saw...it caused me to turn away. Self-hatred can manifest in many ways and prevent you from living a wholesome life. Constantly comparing my looks to others or what their idea of beauty looked like, made me feel inferior and empty inside. Some people would never know I had those issues but guess what...I knew, and so did God. Here are the facts, God knew before I knew, and He knew how deep the emptiness ran in my soul. I could tell myself, "I'm fearfully and wonderfully made and great are His works," but deep down I did not believe it. I had to hit rock bottom so that God could bring me up! Rock bottom for me was a self-loathing spirit!

God is so awesome. He will always place people in your life to encourage you and pull out of you what He placed in you. He will answer all humble prayers of self-improvement because He doesn't want any of His children living in doubt, fear, shame, or have low self-esteem or low self-confidence. He does not want you or me neglecting or dishonoring what He created. He created me, so how could I continue to look at the work He is doing in and through me with disdain? I started asking God to create in me a clean heart...not only for others, but for myself. I asked God to help me like...no love me, and my facial features. I had to stand in the mirror and look at myself, eventually I wouldn't turn away...that's deep!!

Over time, God honored my prayers. He is a God of FREEDOM NOT BONDAGE! My attitude was a form of bondage in my mind and heart. That kind of bondage affects all aspects of your life: mentally, physically, spiritually, and relationally. I was no longer willing to stay bond. Yes, I said willing. You see, we have to choose God and that means all of Him. We MUST choose daily to be free in Christ. God is concerned about our whole temple. It's not just about going to heaven or witnessing to others. It's also about how I carry myself in the day to day events of life. I can't speak empowerment if I'm not empowered myself. I can't say God will deliver and free your mind or we are all beautiful in Christ, if I don't believe it myself. The very life of Jesus represented power and it's not dictated by world views.

There is a physical beauty, but most importantly, we, as Christians should have a spiritual beauty. Once I allowed God to work on my "inner" beauty it flowed to the outside. No, my nose and lips haven't changed, but how I see them has changed because God transformed my mind and heart. I'm a living breathing witness that whatever you place in God's hands, He will either discard or make new. So next time you look in the mirror…listen to what God's voice says about you. Ask Him to open your eyes to see what He sees. Listen to His voice of love and approval. Open your heart to Him and allow the Holy Spirit to make you new and free from the inside out! God's mirror mirror is the only mirror that matters.

Lastly, I would like to share a devotion called the Ultimate Healing Prayer from my book, "Rising Up to Soar". It is based on one of my favorite scriptures, Psalm 103:1-5 (AMP). "Bless and affectionately praise the Lord, O, my soul, And all that is (deep) within me, bless His holy name. Bless and affectionately praise the Lord, O, my soul, And do not forget any of His benefits; Who forgives all your sins, Who heals all your diseases; Who redeems your life from the pit, Who crowns you (lavishly) with lovingkindness and tender mercies; Who satisfies your years with good things, So that your youth is renewed like the (soaring) eagles. When we pray to God, we should always acknowledge His majesty and recognize God's ability to change our lives for the better. God's word is true and gives life to the deadest of dead; and God's love is never ending. He does require your undivided attention and devotion to Him only. God is faithful to give you everything He has promised you according to His word. He will change Your life and desires to match His, and it's all for His glory. Just saying yes to God will open up a world of Kingdom possibilities for your good."

"Father, in heaven, I pray Your blessings upon each and every person that will read the words You have blessed me to write. I pray that their hearts are open to receive Your love and forgiveness leading to eternal life through Christ Jesus. I thank You for sending Your Son to be our Savior. We ask for forgiveness of every sin we have committed. We cast at Your feet every care, worry, doubt, fear and hurt. Transform us by renewing our minds in Christ Jesus. Teach us Your ways and reveal the purpose and plans You have for our lives to bring You glory, for we can do nothing without You. Thank You for being a faithful Father and extending Your grace and mercy towards us daily. May we live in perfect peace, and please You in all that we do. In Jesus' name, Amen."

May God exceedingly and abundantly bless your life as you live whole-heartedly for Him!

#purposeREVEALED #mypinkstilettos

CHAPTER 10

DESPITE THE ODDS

BY STACY BRYANT

I came into the world as an innocent baby. I was picking up bits and pieces of who I am along the way. Each experience was molding and shaping me into the woman I am today. Many of these experiences were positive, but some of them were negative.

At the age of six, I learned that the man who I thought was my father, was not. The father that I knew up to that point was really my stepfather. I did not know the difference until that day.

During my sixth birthday party there was a knock at the door in the middle of the famous "Happy Birthday to you" song. We all got silent as we listened to my father who went to answer the door. We heard voices; then it got louder. The next thing I knew, I saw my father come into the kitchen and grab a butcher knife. We all jumped up to see what was going on, but by the time we got to the door my father and whoever was at the door had moved outside. As they were rumbling in the yard, I remember my mom began to yell and cry. I started to cry as well, and I asked my grandmother, "What is going on?" as tears rolled down my face. My mind wondered, What grudge does this man have against my father?" or vice versa.

She said, "Love, that's your daddy."

I said, "I know but why is he fighting that man."

She said, "No baby, that other man is your daddy."

I cried harder than I ever had before, and I was so very confused. I did not understand what was going on. I had just turned six and my grandmother had just told me that the man I had been calling daddy, my whole life, was not my daddy. And now the daddy, I thought was my daddy was fighting the man who was my true father. How conflicting for a six-year-old to take in. I do not remember much more of that day, except that I cried myself to sleep in my grandmothers' arms after listening to the man who was not my daddy tell the man that was my daddy to never ever come back. That experience started me on a journey of feeling like I never belonged. That experience sent me on an awfully long journey of limited belief in myself and low self-esteem that took me years to comprehend.

From that day forward, I was aware that I was different than my sisters and brother. I felt as if I did not belong, and I honestly believe I was robbed of my innocence. I was robbed of the chance to believe in myself and I had absolutely no clue who I was or where I really came from. I often prayed, "God why?" The years went on, but I felt empty inside. By thirteen, I had developed a relationship with my biological father over the telephone, but still it was not the same. He had missed so much!

My stepfather did provide for the family, but I still walked around feeling as if I did not belong. At twelve, my stepfather gave my mom an ultimatum. The ultimatum was that I had to go or that he would leave. Sadly, my mother gave in to his request, and I moved in with her cousin. Regardless, of this being a sad situation, I started to feel better about things. Then one day, my mother and stepfather came to pick me up a year later. That is when I began being rebellious in hopes that my biological father would come to my rescue.

I began to act out and run away. By the age of fourteen, I was declared by the state as a habitual runaway and placed into a group home. By this time, I was a shell, looking for love in all the wrong places with extremely low self-esteem and getting into trouble in every way possible.

I stayed in the group home about seven months before I was allowed to return home. Once back home, the running away began again, because I just did not feel loved or wanted. Their difference hung in the air like a rain cloud. I would run away, be gone for two or three months, and come back for a warm meal and fresh clothes and then leave again. It was a horrible cycle and I could not seem to break it. I went to a friend's house and had a long talk with her mother. She expressed how she felt about me and how I was a very smart girl, but that I was throwing my life away, living in the streets. I told her that I knew I was smart. When I went to school I made good grades, but it was hard being in school with my home life a wreck. She recommended Job Corp. Although I had never heard of it, she explained that I could go there, get my GED and learn a trade, and at that point be on my own. The being on my own part sounded enticing, so I reached out to a Job Corp recruiter and he signed me up immediately.

I called my mom and told her what I had decided to do and asked if I could come home to stay until it was time to ship out and she agreed. When I got home, I had serious stomach pains, so my mom took me to the emergency room. There, we found out I was pregnant. Wow! I was only fifteen. I was pregnant, yet I was actually happy about it. I felt that I would finally have something that would love me unconditionally; something that would never leave me alone nor would I have to run from it. But my mom and stepfather convinced me to have an abortion. They said, "I was starting a whole new path and that I did not want that extra responsibility." They said, "I was not old enough to care for another human being," so I agreed to the abortion and left to go to Job Corp.

I did exceptionally well and graduated within six months with my GED and a certificate in business. I was ready to start a brand-new life for myself, but because I was only sixteen, things were not as easy as I thought they would be. I could not get anything in my name and people were reluctant to hire me because of my age. Because of this, my life of crime began.

I began selling drugs to make extra cash. It is not something I ever saw myself doing, but what else could I do? McDonalds was just not paying enough, and I thought I needed a quick remedy to my situation. But as soon as I turned eighteen, I hurried and got a job with the telephone company, so that I could retire from my illegal activity.

After working for the telephone company, life got a little simpler. Things calmed down for a little while. But life is life. Traumatic experiences one after the other will simply come out of nowhere. As a child, I was a victim of molestation by four family members. After no one believed me about the first, why bother to seek help with the rest? As an adult, the cycle continued, and I became a victim of rape/sexual assault. Jumping in toxic relationships one after another, and I was searching for my daddy to still come and save me. I soon ended up in an abusive marriage. In an effort to run, I joined the military.

Joining the military seemed to be the best thing for me. An amazing experience. I got to travel and meet new people

--travel abroad to foreign countries, see wars up close, learn new cultures, eat different foods, and be paid all at the same time.

It is amazing how one experience can seem to turn every-thing around. Life before, was not a bowl of cherries. Right as I was swearing in, I had a flashback of all the past painful experiences that I had endured. I thought, I have been given another chance at life...period. I am going to make the best of this. I have no confidence, no self-worth, not even any dis-cipline, but I have been hurt more times than a person could imagine. I endured domestic violence, church hurt, miscar-riages, failed relationships, homelessness, financial despair, mommy issues, daddy issues, and molestation. I thought, okay, here is my chance to leave all of that behind and start life anew.

I mean I really acted like none of It happened. If that is what it took. I will try my best. No one knows me here. They do not know I have no self-esteem. They do not know my ex-husband used to beat me. They do not know that I was loyal to a church that used me for everything. No one in this army even knows that I have been homeless before. They do not know that my body has been through so much that I can barely bear children anymore. They do not know that I do not feel any worth for myself because I cannot maintain a healthy relationship with a man. They do not know that up until now, I have not been financially sound. I get to start my life anew --leaving all of that behind.

No one told me that it is good to start anew, but you never leave anything behind. You really must heal from traumatic experiences.

What? Heal? What is that? Let me just stuff that away. Heal. I would rather just keep it moving. I have a chance to start over; I am about to swear into the military. No one knows me, Here I go.

And that is what I did. I jumped headfirst into the military and served with all my heart. I fell in love with the job and did everything I could to forget about all the traumatic experiences that I had endured before I got there. I decided to make sure I wear the, "Hey, I do not look like what I have been through," so no one will ever know.

Did you know that if you never heal that you keep dragging all that mess around? The past slowly eats away at you. Chip by chip. Bit by bit. Piece by piece. You can only hide it for so long. This story is about me becoming the martyr of my life. A lot of people are not willing to do that. Why? Because they are not even ready to own up to their own part of the process. It is about what everyone else did that caused them to be that way. So healing is almost unreachable. It is like a wine stain on a white rug. It will never go away.

After joining the military, thinking somehow, my life was starting anew, and that magically, I would never experience another traumatic experience, well, the traumatic experiences kept coming. I found myself sexually assaulted again by a leader in my chain of command. I wasted six years in a relationship with someone who did not love me, hoping to finally have someone who did. I found myself in a jump-off relationship, still seeking a love of my own. I was diagnosed with cancer and hid it from everyone for almost two years, in hopes that it would just go away. But after all of the traumatic experiences, I find myself wearing *Pink Stilettos*.

After retirement, I started several businesses and have been really successful at it. Today, that confused little girl is a Retired Veteran, a Master Life Coach Trainer -- who owns a personal development school, and an International Mindset and Manifestation Coach. I'm a radio show host, a bestselling author, and CEO/Founder of a domestic violence nonprofit. I'm a long way away from where I started and a long way away from the experience of traumas on the journey. I have experienced the trauma of molestation, sexual assault, domestic violence, being homeless, toxic relationships and was diagnosed with cancer. A journey of healing and rising from the ashes has not been an easy one. But there are many stories like this one. I am here to show and share that you can go through hell and come back and rise from the ashes.

Because I have walked the road of a survivor my entire life, I am passionate about personal development. I am dedicated to helping others rise above their circumstances. My mission now in life, is to encourage and empower others to explore and find out who they are – inside and out. From there, I believe that they will be able to create the life they have always dreamed of and rise to their full potential, just as I am doing.

I have been through all of this and now I have emerged as pure gold. Wishful thinking --to maintain a balanced life, you must do the work, daily. It is not a one stop shop. I am not this perfect vessel that will never experience another trauma. I must daily evaluate myself, and so should everyone. I must daily put my mental health in check and make sure I am making positive choices and decisions, and so should everyone. I must daily check myself for self-sabotaging behavior, and so should everyone. I must daily affirm to myself who I am and what my purpose is, and so should everyone.

What I hope that someone experiences, while reading the short story of my life, is that despite the odds, you can wear Pink Stilettos!

About Stacy

Stacy Bryant, also known as (Coach Stacy), is the founder of The Stiletto Bosses Network™ and The Free Hope Foundation for Domestic Violence. She is the host of Candid Conversation with Coach Stacy on 108 Praise Radio in Atlanta Georgia. Coach Stacy is also the CEO of ICU Coaching Academy, where she trains and certifies Life Coaches with a passion. She is also known as The Manifest Chic, running the Soul Intention Academy, where she teaches others to master their mindset and manifestations. She is a Retired Veteran of the United States Army and she devotes her life to empowering others. Her goal is to assist and empower people all over the world by instilling and expressing confidence in themselves. Her focus is to empower people by helping them with their finances, relationships, entrepreneurship, health, faith, and life.

Stacy is a Certified Master Life Coach Trainer, author, speaker, and radio personality. Her passion for inspiring and encouraging others has made her a sought-after inspirational speaker and coach. She is the author of "Building Self-Confidence" and the "Her Story" series. Coach Stacy is also the co-author of the "Will to Win" with Brian Tracy. Stacy has a Bachelor's degree in Business Administration and Criminal Justice and is currently pursuing her MBA.

Stacy has walked the road of a survivor her entire life and is passionate about personal development. She is dedicated to helping others rise above their circumstances. Her mission in life is to encourage and empower others to explore and find out who they are –inside and out. From there, she believes they will be able to create the life they have always dreamed of.

CHAPTER 11

THE METAMORPHOSIS

BY TAYLOR J.

Born

Jeremiah 1:5 (KJV) Before I formed thee in the belly I knew thee; and before thou camest forth out of the womb I sanctified thee, and I ordained thee a prophet unto the nations.

B efore a caterpillar is born, it is already predestined to go through a process that will cause it to be completely transformed. The Lord has created you to lead people to Him, so they can be encouraged, inspired, and live a full and abundant life. The process will require you to be resilient, patient, obedient and committed. Are you ready to submit to the process and transformation?

My mother was found in a north St. Louis city dumpster and my father left my mother before he probably knew I existed in her womb. With no history of my bloodline or where I came from, I knew down in my heart that I was called to leave a legacy for my bloodline.

As a young girl only in the fourth grade, I gave my life over to God. I closed my eyes and cried out to God to use me. I remember opening my eyes and I felt lighter than air. The Spirit of God was flowing through me and I knew that I had been changed. My dedication to God was a very serious one for me and I knew that what God had planned for me was very special. What I didn't know was that I would face extremely hard tests and trials that were designed to shape me into who God needed me to be. After that powerful and unforgettable encounter with God, I returned to the women's shelter where my mother and I lived at that time. Growing up in foster care through my teenage years, I didn't have a church home, godly people guiding me, and I did not know to intentionally pursue a relationship with God. All I had was a praying grandmother. I did believe in God and knew that He covered me. Despite rejection, abuse, disappointment, feelings of abandonment and depression, I knew that God would use everything that I was going through to coach people through their process of transformation.

When children hear of their family's history through stories and pictures, they receive a strong sense of belonging, self-worth, and they are more likely to have clarity and direction on what and who they want to become in life.

There is a Quote that states: "One thread alone is weak, but, woven into something larger, surrounded by other threads, it is more difficult to unravel." -Unknown

Belonging to something great makes you feel secure and loved. Many people feel that family goes way beyond bloodlines and last names, but, in fact, that is where your foundation is laid and where God strategically placed you. You are first called to your bloodline. Your family is your first ministry!

When we fall out of the will of God, this inhibits us from truly being intentional with forming godly relationships. As a result, we suffer from dysfunctional broken homes and children who are left without a solid foundation to build upon. This causes a disconnect from your heritage and history, and as a result, you can suffer from identity and abandonment issues.

Despite our mistakes and falling short, God is a Father who loves. He is full of compassion, and most importantly, He sent His only Son to die on the cross for our sins! He is able to turn what was meant for evil into good!

Be Hungry

The female butterfly attaches the eggs to leaves or stems of plants that will also serve as a suitable food source for the larvae when they hatch. When the larvae hatch, their only task is to eat so that they grow into healthy caterpillars.

In 2016, I sat in a jail cell angry, afraid, freezing cold and alone. I cried out for God and there was no answer. I tried to recall scriptures and I couldn't think of any. I sat on the cold metal bed, next to a toilet asking God to come in and save me. My heart was racing; nobody would answer my collect calls. I had no access to the guards. God finally spoke to me, "Taylor, you're going to have to walk this one out. TRUST ME!"

It was that moment when I realized that I'm nothing without His Word! I had no real understanding of who God actually was and who I was in Him. I was terrified, but I knew the first thing I needed to do was get the Word inside of me. I had done lots of great things, but while in that jail cell, I could only truthfully recall one scripture -- St. John 3:16. Did God want me to remember salvation? I spent 12 long hours in that jail cell sitting on a three-inch mattress, in the freezing cold wearing a very thin t-shirt with ONLY that scripture. At that moment, I realized that I seriously needed to be redeemed.

It is important that you continue to feed your spirit by reading the Word of God. Obtain as much knowledge, understanding and wisdom about who God is because when you are tested, you will have to draw strength and instruction from His Word. The more you read and study the Bible, the more you will understand who God is, your identity through Him and what He requires out of your life. This stage is often taken for granted because sometimes we can put busy work before a relationship with Him. God is not appeased by your works. He wants your heart.

This was the beginning of my metamorphosis. Because I suffered from a lack of identity and belonging, I shaped my identity with my works and accomplishments. I learned that my identity is not in my accomplishments or works, but it is in Christ. I am saved by God's grace, not by works! *Ephesians 2:8-9 For by grace you have been saved through faith. And this is not your own doing; it is the gift of God, not a result of works, so that no one may boast.*

The Chrysalis God Is breaking me down!

After wandering for a while looking for a place to transform, the caterpillar finds a safe and sturdy branch or twig and makes a simple silk pad on the underside of it. After that, it uses its cremaster to attach itself to the pad and hangs upside down. Next, it sheds its skin and reveals the chrysalis, and this is where the caterpillar's metamorphosis will take place. Next, the caterpillar releases enzymes that literally break down its own body. During this time, the caterpillar becomes a nutrient rich goo.

I remember waking up freezing on that () three-inch plastic mattress with swollen eyes from crying. The guard was standing in the doorway stating that I needed to follow him. At 1 a.m., I was released! I received my belongings from the jail guard, and he stated that someone would contact me soon. As I walked to my car, I had no idea where my children were. I got into my car, drove home, and sat on the couch in silence. I was about to face the biggest obstacle that I have ever gone through in my life, and it was God who designed it to break me completely down so that He could build me back up again.

During this time, God completely stripped the identity that I created. On the inside, I felt as if my image was destroyed and it caused a pain that I had never experienced before. As a woman who served as a minister, director over the Youth ministry, had a background in social services, successfully aged out of foster care, served on the child abuse and neglect board and above all, was known for having it all together, I felt as if I had failed my bloodline, and most of all, God.

God also stripped me from the support system that I created for myself. The people that I had drawn in close and considered family, actually caused more division among my bloodline. This broke my heart and for the first time in my life, I felt completely alone. In my past, I was able to pull on my network and navigate resources to gain victory, but not this time. Even the system that taught me to navigate resources and advocate for myself was not able to support me.

The chrysalis is dark, and you will feel alone, but remember that even though it feels like a death; you are not in a tomb and God is with you. Tombs are meant for death and God still has more planned for your life. Fear and a lack of faith will cause you to resist and fight God's divine plan. Remember *(2 TIMOTHY 1:7) For God hath not given us the spirit of fear, but of power and of love and of a sound mind.*

(Hebrews 11:1) "Now faith is the substance of things hoped for, the evidence of things not seen."

God Build me back up!

After the caterpillar is completely broken down, at the proper time, the tiny imaginal disks (cells) within the goo begin to form into the butterfly. The beautiful thing about this process is those tiny disks have been within the caterpillar its whole life. Each disk forms a particular part of the butterfly.

After leaving a very important court date, I remember doing about 100 mph down the highway on I-64 going west in the complete opposite direction of home. I was angry because I had just lost in court! I was filled with regret because if I could have spoken up and shared my heart, the judge would have most likely considered ruling in my favor. I remember sitting in the courtroom feeling abandoned and uncovered because everyone had support, but I sat alone. When it was time for me to speak, I froze and felt paralyzed. I looked to my, "soon to be husband" to speak up for me, but he dropped his head. I then looked to my attorney who was there to speak for me, and he said nothing. Before court, I spoke with the both of them, and we discussed the plan, but they failed to follow through. While driving, I realized, I was going in the wrong direction and turned around to head to my business in the city. When I arrived, I remember preparing to enter the building, but instead I decided to rest outside to gather myself. I remember feeling the cool brick on my back and hearing God say, "Trust me."

Over a year later, I woke up one morning and internally I felt as if I was in a deep, cold ditch, naked and exposed. I had nothing and felt like I was at my lowest point. I wasn't working in social services, I wasn't enrolled in school, I wasn't serving in church as a leader, I wasn't running a business, and I wasn't parenting. All of my material things that I worked so hard for were downgraded. God revealed again that my identity is not in my works, positions, titles or the material things that I acquired, but in Him.

2 Corinthians 5:17~ "Therefore, if anyone is in Christ, he is a new creation; old things have passed away; behold, all things have become new."

At the proper time, God will begin to put you back together again. He will first remind you of your first ministry, and that is your family. Despite the mistakes, circumstances and judgements, God has still called you to be a generational curse breaker! Painful circumstances will empower you to shift dramatically and when you do, you will seek God authentically. You will desire His presence and want to get to know who He really is! Extreme pain and suffering will force you to really seek God and find out what your true identity and purpose really is.

Romans 5:3-5 3 Not only so, but we[a] also glory in our sufferings, because we know that suffering produces perseverance; 4 perseverance, character; and character, hope. 5 And hope does not put us to shame, because God's love has been poured out into our hearts through the Holy Spirit, who has been given to us.

During this time, rest in God, get to know who He is through His Word and allow Him to build your character. Find out how much He really loves you and what you truly mean to Him. God will never fail you, leave you, abandon you, mistreat you or inflict any of the pain that people from your past have. The more time you spend building a relationship with God, the more confident you will become in who you are through Him. Learn and embrace your true purpose. According to *(Jeremiah 29:11), For I know the thoughts that I think toward you, saith the Lord, thoughts of peace, and not of evil, to give you an expected end.* Decide to allow God to use you to leave an impact on the future generations in your bloodline.

Emerge

When It's time for a butterfly to emerge, the butterfly has to use its own strength to push the fluids from its body into its wings.

If an outside source assists the butterfly from emerging from the chrysalis, the fluids will never make it into the wings and the wings will remain weak, causing the butterfly to never have the ability to fly.

We often look for outside sources to help us break through but know that you have all that you need.

Emerging requires you to be resilient and have perseverance. You are working and applying what is in you to emerge and it may seem as if you are doing it blindly. This is where you truly have to walk by faith and not by sight!

You have gone through so much up until this point to not have such a press and great emerging! This was designed to cause you to dig deep inside of yourself and utilize everything that God has placed on the inside of you. Trust the voice of God that is instructing you and encouraging you. Every step forward brings forth more divine creativity, wisdom, revelation, and connections. Do not lose faith, remain courageous and become passionate about leaving a legacy for your bloodline!

When you fully emerge, you will be transformed. Everything that was on the inside of you, the pain, the lessons from your obstacles, and all that you have gone through, will be beautifully displayed on your wings. Get ready to fully operate in your purpose and use those beautiful wings to fly!

CHAPTER 12

NEW HORIZON

BY PAMELA KEMP

My walk of life has led me on the path to a spiritual awakening. As a child, I was always inquisitive and questionable about my purpose in life. Unfortunately, the many unanswered questions caused me to feel displaced. During my teenage years, I began to experience deep sadness that left me feeling empty and despondent. Although I was not outgoing, I was known as popular and a laid-back person. Some of my childhood friends would tease me saying, I had ESP. There were times I would randomly speak things that would happen like deja vu. I kept a lot of things bottled up inside of me, but had no problem talking with or helping others sort things out. Even at a young age, people would confide in me and share some of their darkest secrets. I had no idea that God was preparing me for ministry. I did not understand how I was instrumental in people's lives when I was in so much emotional pain myself.

As the emotional pain increased, my soul was becoming more wearied and I found myself isolated from others, including family. I felt I was existing without a purpose. The only thing that gave me joy was my children. I made a vow to God that I would never deny my identity of being a mother. I made a conscious effort to be the best mother I could be. Regardless of what kind of struggles I encountered, I was always conscious of trying to better myself. Whenever I would find the time to be alone, I would journal. This is one of my hobbies. Since I was a young girl, I would talk to God asking many questions. I wanted so desperately for Him to speak to me. I did not know how to discern and hear His voice, but He often showed me things that I knew were not common. I was too embarrassed and afraid to share with others the spiritual things I experienced. My spiritual walk had started to deepen, and I was no longer able to resist the calling on my life. I was always praying and crying secretly; never letting my children see me in distress. After my second child (son) was born, I had a spiritual phenomenon encounter. One night, God came to me in a vision. I felt His presence surrounding the room as I lay in my bed. The light was so radiant and brighter than anything I had ever witnessed. I felt Him clothing me in the garment of peace and wiping away my tears. When the vision was lifted, I asked myself, "What just happened?" I did not share this with anyone for many years.

The second visitation was an enlightenment of my call into the ministry. I was sitting at the kitchen table. I began to feel pressure come over me and my eyes were also getting heavy. Suddenly, I saw myself preaching the gospel on top of a mountain. The background was a beautiful setting of a horizon in the sky. The spiritual transformation was illuminating. Afterwards, I was fearful and was trying to bargain with God not to do this type of ministry work. I did not think I was capable nor qualified to speak, teach, or preach the gospel of Christ. You see, I struggled with insecurities and felt powerless for many years. In 1999, I was ordained into the ministry. The bishop of the congregation ministered to me saying, "God would not have me train through theology school; I was called from my mother's womb and I was highly anointed." The closer I drew to God, the more my faith was challenged. Believe me, at no point in my spiritual walk was I comfortable. However, I obeyed God because I was too afraid of not being in His divine will. When I first started out in the ministry, I would have worship services in my home.

I knew God was seasoning me to step out on faith and resign from my job. Things were becoming more complex and difficult to justify what was going on in my life and my spiritual journey. After stepping out on faith and boldness, all hell broke loose. Not only did people think I was crazy for quitting my job, but some also never believed I was called into the ministry. To make matters worse, I found out I was pregnant with twin daughters after leaving my job; no longer married with two other children. I became a laughingstock and was rejected by many. Comments were made such as God would never call someone in the ministry that was not married and had children. I was ridiculed, ostracized, made fun of, and in some ways disowned. Some of these individuals were close friends and family. I felt like I was dying in the inside. By the time my twins were three years old, I was an emotional basket case. I cried profusely daily, as the hurt manifested into anger. In a matter of a spit second, I went into an emotional outburst that landed me in the hospital. I felt like my heart was cracked in half to the degree I could feel physical pain in my heart. During this episode, my oldest daughter who was only 19 years old at the time was helpful and supportive to me and her siblings.

At the age of 46, I decided to go back to school to earn a college degree. I wanted to set an example for my children to go to college. During my perseverance of being in school, I obtained an associate degree. I continued my education and achieved a bachelor's degree. I remember my mother saying, "Pam, you're going back to school." I said no way, I am sick of school. Well, I found myself right back in school to complete a master's degree. I thought to myself, this is it; I have done enough. Well, there I was back in school in a Doctoral Program. To God be the Glory -- I was finally done with school. The entire time I was in school, I was working a full-time job, in school full time, mentoring children, raising my children, and active in the ministry. I would like to add, each time I completed a degree, God would give me a dream about going to the next level in my education. I knew it was God because He has always dealt with me in dreams and visions. I have a personal and intimate relationship with the Lord.

Out of all the traumatic and horrific things that happened to me, God carried me through. My experience in the hospital was the beginning of my healing process. God went down in the most inner parts of my being and removed pain and hurt that was repressed and suppressed over the years. The devil tried to abort the work God called me to do. The adversary planted seeds of discouragement, doubt, shame, guilt, and disparity. Through it all, I never let go of God's unchanging hand. I learned through my mistakes, but most of all, I gained wisdom. The key to success is walking in "forgiveness." Unforgiveness is unhealthy and can lead to "spiritual cancer." I believe I had to go through these things to testify and tell my story. I minister to many people who are in distress and battling depression. When we lack understanding, we make wrong choices. I profess daily that I am healed, whole, and redeemed through the blood of Jesus.

I never end my day without meditation and writing my daily spiritual affirmations. Before I begin writing, I always invite the Holy Spirit in to help me share words of encouragement. While encouraging others, I am also encouraging myself. Writing helps me with self-awareness and is therapeutic for my entire being. Poems are one of my favorite writings. God has blessed me to have two poems published.

How do we go from brokenness to wholeness? Many people are painfully suffering in their mind, body, soul, and spirit. Unforgiveness and bitterness are roadblocks that prevent healing and deliverance. When we hold onto grudges, we are only hurting ourselves. Forgiveness is imperative to healing. Forgive yourself and others. Integrity reflects our character. If we remain true to ourselves, we do not have to compromise our willingness to be authentic. Beauty starts inwardly and works outwardly. Everybody has a story to tell that has molded them to be the person they are today. No one is perfect because God never intended or created us to be perfect in an imperfect world.

New Horizon

Across the arising heaven there's a horizon sky
The heartbeat of love escalating on high
A melody of music so sweet
Heartfelt love that consumes to the soul to entreat
Many are afraid of unconditional love'
A love that's gentle and pure as a dove
In the center of the wheel is the root of God's plan
Dreams and visions that are articulated
from the master's hand
Deep into the inner of parts of our being
Lie every answer to the simplicity of seeing
Thoughts that are fathomed within one's heart
A painted picture that captures memories
That sometimes seem to separate us apart
Radiating from the explosion of God's beauty
Beaming from the rising of the sun
Searching for zoa vitality that heals the soul
Embracing the serenity that makes us whole
Across the arising heaven there's a new horizon sky

Pamela Kemp

CHAPTER 13

BEAUTIFUL
SCARS

BY DE' IONA MONAY

We impress people with our successes, but we impact them with our scars. Scars tell their own unique story – stories of survival, past mistakes, regrets, and even damage from poor decisions. We all have scars, inside and out. And regardless of how our scars manifested, we need not to feel ashamed but allow the beauty in them to permeate.

For years I found myself wishing my scars would disappear. As a young girl, I was sexually, emotionally, and mentally abused by the men I was supposed to trust most. Although most of my abuse was mental, it led to problems with intimacy, trust, respect, and security within my adult life. The worst part is, it led me to a feeling of "unworthiness." I never believed I was good enough. Why would I? Every man that had entered my life had either hurt and abused me or chose someone else instead of me. At one point in my life, I remember begging a guy to be with me because of how bad I just wanted to be chosen. At times, I would try and force myself to feel thankful for God's "re-direction," but no matter what, I told myself words like "unworthy" and "not enough" were right there swirling in my mind. This was honestly a limiting belief that I never thought I was possible of thinking. But the reality is, limiting beliefs are a lot more common then we think, and that discovery hit me like a ton of bricks. I never resonated with the whole "I am not worthy" story, but unbeknownst to me, it was a scar that had been living deep down inside of me – blocking me from everything I desired. As much as it saddened me that I had these deep-rooted feelings about myself, there was also an instant sense of relief. I realized that those limiting beliefs were only beliefs, not truths.

The truth about unworthiness and any other limiting belief is that it simply isn't real. There are no qualities or characteristics that exclude you from anything that you desire in life. It is a limited way of thinking that prevents you from really putting both feet forward and going for what you want in life. Unworthiness is just our inability to truly love ourselves. Just think about it: if we loved ourselves in a whole and complete way, we would always believe that we could live the life we deserve and have the things we deeply desire. So your ability to achieve your desires, has nothing to do with your worthiness and everything to do with your thoughts, actions, and beliefs. There is nothing more powerful than being the fully-realized you. The world we live in today is all about feeling good or looking a certain way. But the real work is about searching for truth simply because it's YOUR truth. It's about experiencing what is real. And reality includes a canon of experiences that make us all human. It consists of both worthiness and unworthiness.

The first time I felt beautiful with my scars was the day I decided to take ownership of my unworthiness. I took full responsibility for the whispers that I had listened to, believed, and acted upon in my life. Albert Einstein said it best, "we cannot solve our problems with the same thinking we used to create them." So once I identified and acknowledged my limiting belief – I was finally able to move beyond it.

After acknowledging the source of my scars, I began a daily meditation practice speaking to the opposite of my limiting beliefs. I had to experience myself without limits. I had to be open to feeling what it was like to be my true self. I found it helpful to write down my negative thoughts, and for every negative word, I would write a positive alternative next to it. If I started to feel overwhelmed with the aspect of "positive thinking," I would start with just one area of my life and focus my thoughts there. This was a cornerstone of my healing journey. Meditation helped me sift through my mind and discover patterns of thought. As you begin recognizing patterns of thinking, you will be able to see which streams of thoughts you are habitually feeding with your attention. I had to reprogram my mind and replace any limiting beliefs with new powerful beliefs of myself. I had to get intentional about how I wanted to think, act, and feel. When you get clear on how you want to feel, the thoughts behind those feelings help bring those manifestations into reality. We can write a thousand lists and make a million vision boards, but if we don't clearly feel what we want to experience, it will never truly manifest itself. We must make time for contemplating, thinking, feeling, and believing. Meditation is all about letting thoughts come and go rather than consciously directing them toward a particular result.

Through my journey of healing, I also discovered visualization activities which helped me tremendously. It might sound counterintuitive to combine visualization and meditation, but they actually go hand-in-hand. When you visualize, you focus on something specific such as an event, person, or goal you want to achieve, then you hold it in your mind and imagine your outcome becoming a reality.

Visualization is one of my favorite meditation techniques. I have used the art of visualization to create some beautiful experiences in my life. I remember the summer of 2016 – I manifested my dream vehicle that I had on my dream board for four years. Last year I even manifested a trip to Africa! I literally took a random photo off of the internet, imagined I was there, felt the feeling of being there, and not even six months later, I was standing in the exact spot the photo was taken. Manifestation affords you the ability to create the outcome of an event before it has happened. It's a superpower that we all possess. Don't take my word for it; ask Superstar-athlete and the all-time leader in medals won at the Olympics, Michael Phelps. He employs visualization as part of his winning strategy. For months before a race, Michael mentally rehearses for two hours a day in the pool. He sees himself winning. He smells the air, tastes the water, hears the sounds, sees the clock, and imagines himself crossing the finish line before everyone else. It has been proven that both meditation and visualization used together can be a very powerful tool in changing the course of your life. If Mike and I can improve our circumstances and manifest our way to winning – so can you!

Although emotional pain heals slowly, as I have been slow to heal, my healing did not begin until I decided my scars were beautiful. That's when I became beautiful. When I took power away from the negative emotions, I was better able to find joy in the present. There is our brokenness in the physical sense, such as breaking an arm or leg that may require surgery. On the contrary, there is spiritual brokenness that will always require surgery of the soul. Scars not only tell the story of past wounds, but they tell the story of healing. Because if there were no scars, there would be no healing. A scar only appears in the wake of healing. A wound that was once open but has now closed. Healing has taken place and has left its mark as a scar. I now see scars as stories. I see a person who has lived, who has depth, and who is a survivor. Living is beautiful & it is beautiful to have really lived, and have the marks to prove it. It's not a competition as in "my scar is better than your scar," but it is a testament to our inner strength.

Opening up emotional scars in order to heal from them takes an immense amount of courage. Making the decision to confront these underlying emotional wounds and face them head-on can be an intimidating process. Two of the most important things you can do throughout this journey is to practice self-love and patience. There are days when I feel like my progress moves one step forward and two steps backward, but if dealing with emotional scars was easy, they would not be called emotional scars. It's a complicated process, so be sure to give yourself the benefit of the doubt on tough days. Especially on those days when you're frustrated with your progress – self-love and kindness are key. Celebrate the progress you have made regardless of how small it may seem. You have been conditioned to believe that you are the problem. You are not and never have been the problem. All you need to do is begin to look inside yourself and become empowered as your own solution. There is always an internal resolution for anything that is happening in your life externally. See, there is a multi-dimensional nature to life. We are more than the roles that we play. You have the capacity to exist beyond what you have been told, beyond how you have been programmed, and beyond what you have been conditioned to see. You are more than a set of reactions. You are more than all of your possessions. You are more than your profession. You are a pure being with the capacity to do anything you set your mind to. You are awareness and peace. Love yourself and remember your scars are beautiful!

"Scars Are Indication Of Where You Come From, Not A Limitation To Where You Are Going"
~Larita Rice-Barnes~

CHAPTER 14

WHERE ARE THE TAMARS?

BY GALE MC KOY-GEORGE

t is evident that as mothers, parents, and caregivers, we are being called to be vigilant and alert regarding sexual molestations and sexual abuse.

WHO WAS TAMAR?

Tamar was a young virgin princess, the daughter of King David who was raped, despised, rejected, and left to live a lonely life in her brother Absalom's house. The account of this can be found in 2 Samuel 13. It reveals a family secret that later turned very tragic.

The story gives an account of a daughter and sister being raped and asked to be silent for now by her brother Absalom. This statement resembles our modern-day stories where women are asked to be SILENT against their perpetrators and rapists even though they are the victims. The father, King David, on the other hand, was enraged by the incident but refused to punish his son Amnon for his wrongdoing. This is not different in our today's world. Many perpetrators (men) are not being held accountable for their sexual wrongdoings. And finally, among others, the account where Absalom said nothing good or bad for two years; he was silent. Perhaps he was planning his revenge to take over his father's throne.

My question today to those that are reading is, how could this tragic story have ended differently? How can we play a vital role in preventing this from happening again? And how can we reach those who have fallen prey to the hands of rapists?

THE AFTERMATH

This was the story of Tamar's place of destitution. The Bible says, "So his servant put her out and bolted the door after her. She was wearing an ornate[a] robe, for this was the kind of garment the virgin daughters of the king wore. 19 Tamar put ashes on her head and tore the ornate robe she was wearing. She put her hands on her head and went away, weeping aloud as she went." Her brother Absalom saw her and asked, "Is it true that Amnon has been with you? Well, my sister, keep quiet for now, since he's your brother. Don't you worry about it." So, Tamar lived as a desolate woman in her brother Absalom's house. 2 Samuel 13:18-20 (NIV).

WHAT IS RAPE?

The Merriam Webster dictionary describes rape as an "unlawful sexual activity, and usually, sexual intercourse carried out forcibly or under threat of injury against a person's will or with a person who is beneath a certain age or incapable of valid consent because of mental illness, mental deficiency, intoxication, unconsciousness, or deception."

My question to you in the content of the definition is, have you been raped, and secondly have you gotten over it?

AROUND THE WORLD

"South Africa has the highest rate of rape in the world of 132.4 incidents per 100,000 people. According to a survey conducted by the South African Medical Research Council, approximately one in four men surveyed, admitted to committing rape." (world population review, 2020).

The United States has a rape rate of 27.3. As in many other countries, rape is grossly underreported in the United States due to victim shaming, fear of reprisal, fear of family knowing, cases not being taken seriously by law enforcement, and possible lack of prosecution of the perpetrator. Only 9% of rapists in the US get prosecuted, and only 3% of rapists will spend a day in prison. 97% of rapists in the United States will walk free." (world population review, 2020).

LET'S TALK ME

God has given us the mandate to protect, cover, and nurture those that he has placed in our care. I have had the opportunity so many times to listen and walk many through the process of restoration after being raped, abused, or sexually assaulted.

I myself, was a victim of sexual assault as a teenager and had never spoken, reported, or addressed the incident until I was a grown woman when the Holy Spirit reminded me of what happened. I was shocked that I had buried and forgotten the incident for over 22 years. The recollection of the incident out of the blue was an eye-opener to me. When I walk people through their place of freedom, I am always open and sensitive when they indicate that they had forgotten what really happened to them when they were raped or sexually assaulted. I came to understand that the mind is so strong and yet so weak. It has the ability to reveal and conceal vital information that can keep you in bondage and or can set you free.

I must say that I had totally forgotten that I had that encounter in my life. In retrospect, I know that the hands of God really navigated me through that place to forget it all. I had amnesia of the incident for 22 long years. For many, it might not have been or will be their story. But the crucial thing of sexually assaulted or rape victims is that they need their souls to be fixed and healed, and only JESUS can do so.

God can transcend years of pain, suffering, shame, bondage, and restore someone to their original purpose and intent of God. Even though God has allowed the blood of Jesus to be shed upon the cross to redeem us back to him, it is not by force. He will not override our freedom to choose. That will be our responsibility to take advantage of the grace of God that has been given to us. The Bible says in John 10:10 (NIV), "The thief comes only to steal and kill and destroy; I have come that they may have life and have it to the full". The father's intent for us is to live in the freedom, and that was given to us when Jesus paid the price on the cross of Calvary.

Please do not get me wrong. In the process of us doing so, we may miss the mark and may not see all that needs to be seen, not being able to care for all that needs to be cared for. But one thing is evident; we need to be vigilant. The Bible says, "Be alert and of sober mind. Your enemy, the devil, prowls around like a roaring lion looking for someone to devour (1Peter 5:8 NIV). We need to look out for those around and among us, your children, both male, and female.

When we look at the story of Tamar, we realize that people can be raped, sexually assaulted, and defiled and never recover from it if it's not dealt with care, sensitivity, and wisdom. The Bible said Tamar was left destitute. 2 Samuel

13:20. When we look at the word DESTITUTE, "it means extremely poor and lacking the means to provide to oneself, not having. (Dictionary.com).

This famous story of Tamar's defilement has caused many other ripple incidents to occur because it was not dealt with properly. Because King David did not address the incident with wisdom and sensitivity, many things happened as a result.

1. Absalom, Tamar's brother, asked her to be silent about the incident. (2 Samuel 13:20)

2. There was bloodshed, where Absalom killed the rapist, his half-brother Amnon. (2 Samuel 13:29).

3. Absalom stole the heart of the people and attempted to take over the throne from his father, the King. (2 Samuel 15:6).

4. The premature death of Absalom. (2 Samuel 18:15)

"It is estimated that approximately 35% of women worldwide have experienced some form of sexual harassment in their lifetime. In most countries with data available on reported rape cases, less than 40% of women who experience sexual violence seek help. Less than 10% seek help from law enforcement" (world population review, 2020).

My prayer is that this chapter will provoke you to become alert and watchful for your children, those in your care, and those around you. We cannot allow the princess and virgins of the kingdom to be left unattended and mentally and emotionally handicapped, living like zombies in the world of isolation. We have got to reach out to those that have been wounded and left for dead. We have got to pour in the oil and the wine, the healing of God into their wounded souls, and bring them back to life again.

The Bible says the strong must help the weak. So those of us that have been strengthened, let us strengthen those who need us now.

So, to all the Tamars in isolation, we are calling you out. You no longer must be in destitution. Jesus paid the price all for you, and He has sent us to bring you out again. You are royalty and were created and called forth from darkness to show forth His marvelous light and the beauty of God. (1 Peter 2:9).

So, it is time to arise and shine. We believe in you that you can make it. The destitute places have been closed, the hiding holes have been opened, and your place at the table has your name tag on it. Only you can sit there. Healing and restoration are your portions, "for this purpose was the Son of God made manifest......1 John 3:8. Hallelujah.

CHAPTER 15

KEEP ON KEEPING ON

BY SHAMILA RAMJAWAN

I am Shamila Ramjawan, a 56-year-old South African woman. I am a philanthropist, Mrs. Johannesburg 2019, multiple global awardee and speaker, Brand South Africa Play Your Part Ambassador, a University of South Africa Business Management Lecturer, Ladies of All Nations International South Africa Chairperson, and the Founder of the PrincessD Menstrual Cup, a division of Famram Solutions.

When I was 34 years old, my husband who was a Detective Sergeant with the South African Police Services, had a sudden heart attack and died. This left me as a young widow to fend for myself and take care of my two young children as a single parent. I then decided to continue with my studies to elevate myself and climb the corporate ladder. To date, I have a Master in Business Administration (MBA), among many other qualifications, and I am currently a doctoral candidate. I found that to grow and develop, I had to educate myself to a level of being unstoppable.

In 2014, I decided to take the plunge and left the corporate world to become an entrepreneur. I started Famram Solutions, a marketing company.

Having worked with communities for over a decade, I realized there was a dire need to research the menstrual cup as an affordable solution for menstruation. Most girls in rural areas miss school for up to 7 days in a month because of this. In 2016, I launched the PrincessD Menstrual Cup. It is cost-effective, eco-friendly and hygienic; an ideal solution to keep girls in school because its reusable for 10 years. I have changed the lives of thousands of girls and women with this sustainable sanitary product which is available in over 20 countries.

As Nelson Mandela once said, "Education is the most powerful weapon you can use to change the world." I believe in "keeping girls in school." My solution to keeping girls in school is by providing them with a sustainable solution for menstruation.

The major challenge that I faced was finding the right support network with the adjustment from corporate to being an entrepreneur. My MBA degree was a tool to overcome and ease into the transition. I started by latching onto women-focused networking events. I persevered to create visibility of my brand despite having the fears of failure; so I never gave up.

I own my success by sharing my trials and tribulations to other entrepreneurs. Success is achieved by hard work, determination and being disruptive as we grab opportunities that come by. I recently created a platform, Red Corner Chat, my own talk show to engage with others so that they, too, can inspire and motivate others by sharing their stories. My mantra is "Believe in yourself and Dream Big."

My contribution towards this book is believing in the power of pink and to evoke solidarity with women who experience the painful and stressful trauma of breast cancer.

As C.S. Lewis states, "Hardships often prepare ordinary people for an extraordinary destiny." I believe that you have the power to overcome all obstacles in life no matter how bad the situation is.

It is important to remember that God has plans for all of us. It is His doing to put you through this temporary situation. God gives His strongest battles to people like you. He knows that it is you that will fight these battles and rise to be the giant that you always wanted to be. He knows that you will be the one that is courageous to share your story so that you, too, can help and encourage others to overcome their pain and traumatic experiences.

When faced with adversity in life, you may ask the question, "Why me?" The reality is that people everywhere are facing problems that they see as difficult and stressful as well. I lost my husband at a young age and became a widow. I still strived through all adversities to be a better person and focused on myself and my children. I was resilient and took many business risks and my journey has been one of consistently breaking barriers. I use my inspiring life story to help individuals unleash their true potential. So, remember, you are not alone but it's just that you are fighting a different battle.

Embrace your life, take your time to manage your stress and emotions, practice gratitude more than hating your life; stay close to your feelings, even the most painful ones and accept success and failure as part of your life's journey. You are a winner and you will rejoice as you grow into this grand storyteller.

I am sorry that you are going through this, but this, too, shall pass. Believe in yourself and believe in the power of prayer. I would love for you to share your story to inform and inspire others on my chat show, "Red Corner Chat," which is a global platform. Together, we can impact the lives of people anywhere around the globe.

Nobody will ever realize your struggle until you disclose your story. Be the one to comfort others by talking about your hardships and your journey no matter what it is. It will surely inspire others and create awareness that there are opportunities out there where they can grab and steer their own ship to success. Never ever give up.

Your messages to the world must be words of encouragement, motivation, and inspiration always. If you live it, share it.

CHAPTER 16

LIFE IS BEAUTIFUL

BY ADRIJA BISWAS

L ife is like a boxing ring – defeat is not declared when you fall down, but it is declared when you refuse to get up – Rise and Shine again!

Have you ever had moments when you didn't know your purpose in life?; when you felt life was a chore?; when you felt you were not good enough?; and you felt, "Why Me?" Life will always throw challenges your way. There will be pains and there will be hurts, but no matter, these setbacks do not have to stop you. You can always re-create your stories and make your life beautiful again.

There are people today that have a successful career and a happy life. But what lies beneath is a range of experiences from being a 9/11 survivor to creating precedence in Indian law. I have not just seen ups and downs, but summits and valleys. I have had first-hand experience of women giving up on hope, struggling through challenges, losing the will to live and then rebounding back from their lowest points. My friends ask me how I manage to stay positive in life and how do I continue to see the beauty and good in others.

The color pink is the color of universal love of oneself and of others. Pink represents friendship, affection, harmony, inner peace, and approachability. When I was approached to be a part of this Pink Stilettos book project, it was the perfect way to tell others just how human I really am and how we all are. Truly we are capable of incredible things – irrespective of our past and challenges.

Self-Care: Love yourself and choose your association

Even when we are on an aircraft, we have heard the flight attendant say, "In case of an emergency put on your oxygen mask first, before you can assist others. It's the same with life. We need to look after ourselves first – not just our physical health, but our mental, emotional and spiritual wellbeing. Your health is what you feed yourself, feed your mind, and feed your soul. The more positive and healthy emotions you intake, the more positive and healthy emotions you will radiate. Self-care and self-love are not just a personal and holistic transformation for yourself, but in the process, your aura and positive vibes will transform people around you, too.

Surround yourself with people that motivate you, believe in you, and support you through thick and thin.

My Motto - Surround yourself with people who lift you and bring the best out in you.

You have heard of the famous saying of the glass filled with water, "glass half full" referring to an optimist and, "glass half empty" referring to the pessimist. But for me "my glass has always been full" – half with water and half with air. This, my friends, I like to call the "Positive Mindset" one of the key factors of success.

Positive Mindset

Positivity does not mean that you have to always be happy and smiling. Positivity does not mean that you will not have challenges because you wish for positive things to happen. Positivity is more around your perception and perspective on life, people and things around you and your attitude to focus on all the good things in people and things. We are all in different "boats," but we are all facing similar storms in our day to day lives. Each one of us have different styles, attitude, resilience and ways of coping and reacting to these challenges. If we made ourselves strong and resilient with a positive attitude and focused on the positive outcomes, we will be able to make our lives beautiful.

There is a beautiful story about a potato, an egg and coffee beans going through the same adversity of boiling water and how each one reacted differently. The potato went in strong but in boiling water became soft and weak. The egg was fragile, but with the boiling water the inside of the egg became hard. The coffee beans changed the water and created something new. What will you be?

My motto - Don't tell yourself your life is difficult, tell your difficulties, you are difficult!!

CHAPTER 17

A GIRL WITH A DIFFERENT WORLD AND BIG THOUGHTS

BY HENA PAYGHAM

am Hena Paygham, a girl with a different world, big thoughts, liberal, strongly opposed to patriarchy and violence against women. I remember from the time I was very young, I could not stand the inequality and oppression of a woman in front of my eyes. When I saw a man oppressing a woman or preventing her from working and studying outside the house, I would lock myself in a room. I would cry and a fire lit up in me. How can I prevent all this?! This stayed with me until I became a teenager and finished school. There was something else in me since that time pulling me towards it.

When I was a child, I had other dreams, but suddenly I had a feeling that in the country where I lived, there are very few people who are honestly the voice of the people, and I had to be one of them. Although I was only sixteen years old, I made the biggest decision of my life and flipped through the most important page of my life. I got into the journalism field. I started writing for women's empowerment. I started working as a feminist and I started to raise my voice against the mistakes made in the name of religion. As a journalist, writer, and feminist, I set a goal to present the truth to the world without any fear or censorship. I accepted the possibility of my death, but I am not willing to stand in front of the camera or hold a pen in my hand to support a specific religion, person or something unjust.

I was born into a Muslim family but I am strongly opposed to Islamic thought. Since I always tell the truth and I do not support a religion and I do not like to wear hijab forcefully, and I like to live freely, some extremist people are so opposed to me that they warned me to wear hijab and not raise my voice against their activities. But I did not take all this seriously, and I was getting stronger every day. In those days, I created a page for women empowerment called Voice of Women on social media. But after creating this page, the threat and activities of some extremists became so much against me, that they made it difficult for me to work in the media and writing. So much so, that my family and I were forced to move to another country to live a peaceful and secure life. So, my family and I left Afghanistan, and went to India because India is a democratic country and I could raise my voice freely. There, we became refugees. While living in Afghanistan, the only sentence I heard from everyone was that you could not do anything in India or another country as a refugee. But "you can't" was the sentence that changed my life.

Because I was in the air of "touching the skies," I started working hard non-stop, and I was able to make the impossible turn possible!! My articles were published in national and international magazines and newspapers. Although I was only twenty years old, I was selected as the global ambassador to one of the international organizations, my biography was published in one of the international books among the influential figures of the world, I was selected the youngest Goodwill Ambassador to another international organization. I received the title of Global Change Maker from one of the world's most prestigious organizations. I also won the title of the most active and youngest woman in the world. I was selected as the project head in many projects and I was able to provide a platform for women to reach out to the world under different titles, I also was selected the national president and faculty member in one of the international universities, I was selected as an expert panelist for Speak Up and Empower Women. But all this is not enough for me. My path continues. And the air of touching the skies makes me more impatient every day. I will be the voice of every woman from all over the world. I will be a role model for my generation. I will be a picture of hope not a picture of war and misery.

No matter what backward country you are from, when you have the will and make the effort to succeed, you will reach the pinnacle of success. Because our lives are made by our thoughts, not by our place of birth and religion.

*"Testimonies DON'T Expire
Who Told YOU To Stop Telling
Your Story"
~Larita Rice-Barnes~*

Made in the USA
Monee, IL
26 November 2020